D0814107

ABRAHAM

ABRAHAM
ONE
GOD
THREE
WIVES
FIVE
RELIGIONS

FRANCES WORTHINGTON

Bahá'í
PUBLISHING
Wilmette, Illinois

Bahá'í Publishing
415 Linden Avenue, Wilmette, Illinois 60091-2844
Copyright © 2011 by the National Spiritual Assembly of
the Bahá'ís of the United States

All rights reserved. Published 2011
Printed in the United States of America on acid-free paper ∞

14   13   12   11   4   3   2   1

Library of Congress Cataloging-in-Publication Data

Worthington, Frances.
  Abraham : one God, three wives, five religions / Frances Worthington.
    p. cm.
  Includes bibliographical references and index.
  ISBN 978-1-931847-89-6 (acid-free paper)
  1. Abraham (Biblical patriarch) 2. Abrahamic religions. I. Title.
  BS580.A3W63 2011
  222'.11092—dc23
                              2011023464

Cover design by Andrew Johnson
Book design by Patrick Falso

For John

ACKNOWLEDGMENTS

A question about Muḥammad and Abraham asked by Christopher Henderson, then age fourteen, was the hook that tugged me into the story of Abraham. Shahin Borhanian and Professor Richard Thomas were the first to suggest that it was time to write a book. My good friend Jan Ray cheered the project on with unfailing enthusiasm. The patient attention and probing questions of a group of students who signed up for my course on Abraham in the fall of 2008 through the Osher Lifelong Learning Institute at Furman University influenced the organization of the chapters, though they might not have realized it at the time. Dr. Michael Gauderer was kind enough to translate an article from "Der Spiegel."

An angelic host of collaborators from several different religions provided invaluable assistance by reading various incarnations of the manuscript and courageously providing sharp and very helpful feedback. They include Carol Ann Heymann, Samir Jaber, Dr. Fred Leffert, Tariq Rashid, Liz Rose, Shaun Stone, Al Tompkins, and Shahin Vafai, plus fellow members of the Women's Interfaith Book Club: Dorcus Abercrombie, Bonita Bost, JoAnn Borovicka, Carolyn Dicer, Rev. Dr. Michelle McClendon, Rev. Julie Schaff, Mareon Stall, and Louise Tajuddin. Christopher Martin, working from his lair deep in the heart of Texas, introduced me to the paperless process of computer-assisted editing and patiently polished the chapters one by one.

CONTENTS

Contents

LIST OF ILLUSTRATIONS AND MAPS

2011 MAP WITH MODERN BOUNDARIES
PLUS ANCIENT CITIES OF UR AND HARRAN

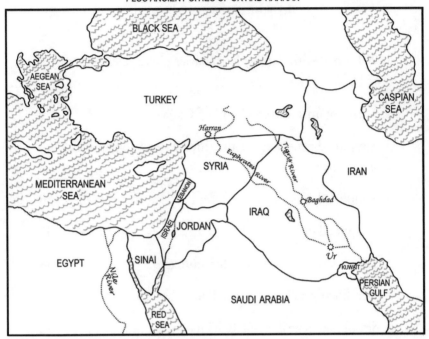

MESOPOTAMIA AND THE LAND OF CANAAN C. 2,000 BC

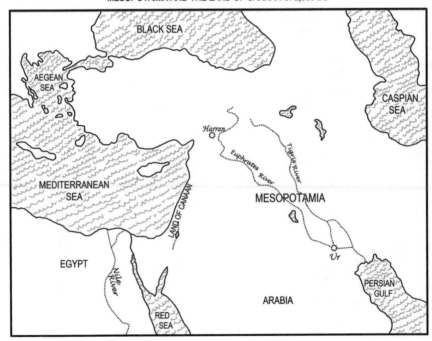

Simplified genealogy
of the three wives/concubines of Abraham

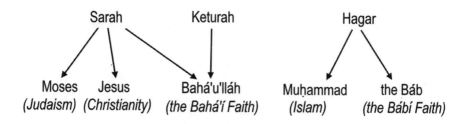

Sarah   Keturah   Hagar

Moses Jesus   Bahá'u'lláh   Muḥammad   the Báb
(Judaism) *(Christianity)* *(the Bahá'í Faith)* *(Islam)* *(the Bábí Faith)*

ABRAHAM

PROLOGUE

Anyone foolhardy enough to contemplate adding another volume to the already towering stack of books about Abraham ought to have a rationale, so here is mine: Although the story of Abraham and the three wives / concubines who birthed five religions is a spiritual soap opera that's been running for about four thousand years, very little has been written about it from the perspective of someone who is a member of the newest of the Abrahamic religions—the Bahá'í Faith. This book doesn't represent the opinion of every Bahá'í, and it's not an official statement. It's just what I see when I squint my eyes and gaze into the past.

In writing from a Bahá'í viewpoint, I build on three basic assumptions:

- Abraham was a Messenger of God Who lived about four thousand years ago and established the concept of monotheism.
- Each of the five religions alluded to in the title of the book—Judaism, Christianity, Islam, the Bábí Faith, and the Bahá'í Faith—is an important and legitimate chapter in the overarching book of divine knowledge.
- The Founders of these religions (Moses, Jesus, Muḥammad, the Báb, and Bahá'u'lláh) are descendants of Abraham via the three wives / concubines that are mentioned in the Book of Genesis: Sarah, Hagar, and Keturah.

The most important sources of information for this exploration of Abraham have been the sacred texts of the Abrahamic religions:

- The Tanakh of Judaism, which is also referred to as the Old Testament

- The New Testament of Christianity
- The Qur'án of Islam
- The writings of the Báb in the Bábí Faith
- The sacred and authoritative writings of the Bahá'í Faith

Each religion has something special to say that enriches our understanding of who Abraham was and what His effect on history has been. In addition, I've delved into stories about Abraham contained in the oldest traditions of Judaism, Christianity, and Islam, and have had a wonderful time perusing books of history, geography, archaeology, and even poetry at various public and university libraries.

The real miracle in this effort, however, has been the World Wide Web. Prior to this incredible era of computer-aided search, it would have been well-nigh impossible to unearth the disparate nuggets of information needed to construct this narrative.

Much of the excitement of researching the Abrahamic soap opera has come from discovering unexpected connections between the widely-spaced episodes. With each twist and turn of the plot, I've been forced to reevaluate prior assumptions and reassess evidence. What seemed true at the beginning was sometimes proven false by something discovered much later. In probing the various levels of meaning in scriptural verses, I've been guided by the belief that science and religion are God-given partners. Each is dedicated to a certain kind of truth, each can inform the other, and both are essential to a balanced understanding of our spiritually physical (or physically spiritual) universe.

On the few occasions when it has been necessary to reconcile conflicting information from different religions, I've adhered to two basic rules:

- When scripture and tradition disagree, scripture wins.
- When old and new scripture disagree, the scripture from the most recent Revelation takes precedence because it is the newest Word of God.

This book is not a work of fiction because I've remained within the bounds of what is indicated by a combination of scriptural text, historical data, and archaeological evidence. Nevertheless, for the sake of readability and just plain fun, the storyline is delicately dusted with the tasty spices of *probably* and *possibly*.

As I write these words, my ears are buzzing with the strident summer song cicadas use to attract a mate. My laptop and I are crouched on the sofa of a small room near the soft beach that clothes the outer edge of Kiawah Island, South Carolina. The room is on the second floor, but the greater part of the view to the horizon is blocked by a tangle of live oaks and scrambling muscadine vines. All I can see of the sky are a few tantalizing shimmers of blue, the perfect metaphor for my attempts to peer beyond the thicket of prior assumptions and take a fresh look at the Father of Monotheism.

NOTE TO THE READER

Bahá'ís believe in God, Who has created the universe and all that dwell therein. God has, with abundant grace, provided spiritual and moral guidance to mankind through a series of divine Prophets, including Muḥammad, Jesus, Buddha, Moses, and Abraham. The most recent divine Messenger, Bahá'u'lláh, founded the Bahá'í Faith in 1863. Bahá'u'lláh's coming was foretold in 1844 by the Báb, Who was martyred for His beliefs in 1850. The central purpose of the Bahá'í Faith is the establishment of the oneness of humanity, and its millions of adherents come from virtually every tribe, race, and nation in the world.

Throughout this book, several different words are used to denote the Messengers of God, including *Prophet, Messenger, Messiah, Revelator,* and *Manifestation.* Bahá'ís make a distinction between Messengers such as Jesus and Muḥammad, who were anointed by God for the specific purpose of bringing a new Revelation to mankind, and minor prophets such as Isaiah and Job, who revitalized peoples' faith but did not establish a new religion.

Also, as a sign of respect, all of the personal pronouns referring to the Messengers of God are capitalized.

To make it easier to remember exactly where a certain city or country is or was, modern place names are often used when an older name might be more accurate—and vice-versa. Thus, for instance, Canaan, Palestine, and Israel are used interchangeably throughout the book, even though each term is appropriate to a different era and each is associated with slightly different boundaries.

1

ON THE MOVE

And recite to them the story of Abraham.
Muhammad[1]

Four thousand years ago, Abraham was alive and on the move, though not voluntarily. He had been banished from Iraq for preaching monotheistic ideas that angered the local polytheistic priesthood and was headed toward Israel, where He would make a new life and establish a group of followers who would remember Him and try to follow His teachings. Or, to describe it in biblical terms, Abraham was traveling away from Ur of the Chaldees, intent on reaching the Land of Canaan.

In seeking to share a new religious message, Abraham was following in the noble footsteps of several of His prophetic ancestors, including Enoch and Noah, who had also been active in the Middle East. During His life, Abraham would face rejection, danger, and banishment; but, precisely because He was willing to sacrifice His own comfort and follow God, He would also be the recipient of divine blessings. Over the course of four thousand years, His descendants, born of three different women, would give rise to several religions and cause Abraham's name to be revered throughout the world.

Creating an exact timeframe for the events of Abraham's life would be a wonderful thing, but His date of birth remains elusive.

For the purposes of this book, a date of roughly 2000 BC will suffice, though there are legitimate arguments for setting it as early as 2158 BC or as late as the year that is honored by Jewish tradition: 1812 BC.

Whatever Abraham's date of birth, the scene of His nativity is generally agreed to be somewhere in southern Iraq, along the course of the Euphrates River. Due to historical changes in terminology, this area has been described in several different ways. Islamic traditions refer to the setting as Babylon. The Bahá'í writings say Abraham was born in Mesopotamia, a large area that includes southern Iraq and a smidgen of Iran, along with slices of Turkey and Syria. The Old Testament description joins the name of what was once a well-known city (Ur) to the name of a powerful tribe (the Chaldeans), producing the name that is written in the Book of Genesis: *Ur of the Chaldees* or, in some translations, *Ur of the Chaldeans.*[2]

LOCATING UR

The city of Ur itself, which lay within the heart of the region referred to as *Ur of the Chaldees,* is the site most often suggested as the place where Abraham was born. Situated at the edge of the Euphrates River, about two hundred miles south of where Baghdad is today, it was one of the most cosmopolitan metropolises of the world. Within its protective walls lived as many as sixty-five thousand people, some of them wealthy enough to wear lapis lazuli necklaces of the deepest blue, drink from silver cups, eat from alabaster bowls, and hire servants to do most or all of the household work.

But, tempting as the city of Ur is, there are several arguments against believing that it was the site of Abraham's birth. The first argument doesn't negate Ur as a choice but simply points out that the term *Ur of the Chaldees* refers to the whole region, which included dozens of towns and villages where Abraham's parents might have lived.

Another argument against the city of Ur is based on a verse in the Book of Joshua that indicates that God brought Abraham to

Israel from "the other side of the flood."[3] Interpreting "flood" as "Euphrates" because the river was famous for its seasonal floods, and looking at geography from Israel's perspective (which is where Joshua was living), Joshua's finger seems to point not to the city of Ur, located on the west side of the river, but to the land on the "far" or eastern side of the river. On the other hand, the verse may be a purely metaphorical description of the way in which Abraham's Revelation succeeded Noah's, because Noah was before the flood and Abraham was after it, or "on the other side."

Yet another strike against the metropolis of Ur lies in Jewish tradition, which names the place of Abraham's birth quite specifically as the town of Kutha (also spelled *Cuthah*). Located about forty miles south of modern Baghdad, Kutha is positioned "on the other side of the flood" because it is on the east bank of the Euphrates. And, as a clincher, one of the tells within its boundaries has Abraham's name attached to it.[4]

Tell, meaning *tall* or *hill*, is a word that has been used for centuries to refer to mounds of rubble from ancient settlements that were destroyed or abandoned because of the catastrophic effects of earthquakes, floods, and war—not to mention plagues, shifting riverbeds, and wells that ran dry. To differentiate one tell from another, local residents have habitually added a descriptor referring to a memorable event, a famous resident, or the original name of the collapsed village. Tell Basta in Egypt, for instance, was once the home of the cult of the cat-goddess Bastet. And Tell Ibrahim at Kutha (*Ibrahim* is the Arabic transliteration of *Abraham*) got its name because of its historical connection to the life of Abraham— or at least that's the theory.

Perhaps somewhere in an as-yet-unexcavated ruin lies a clue whose retrieval will dispel the mysteries surrounding Abraham's birth and settle the issue. Meanwhile, we are forced to be content with knowing that in a city, town, village or encampment along the Euphrates—we'll call it Ur while agreeing that it might not be—a very important baby was born.

A KING'S NIGHTMARE

The prospect of welcoming a baby into the world, especially a male, was generally a cause for celebration in Mesopotamia. But for the local king, known as Nimrod, the impending birth of Abraham was a nightmare. Bahá'í scripture outlines the story this way: "Among the Prophets was Abraham, the Friend of God. Ere He manifested Himself, Nimrod dreamed a dream. Thereupon, he summoned the soothsayers, who informed him of the rise of a star in the heaven."[5]

Jewish tradition explains that the rise of the star signaled the birth of a child who would forever change the way religion was practiced.[6]

At that time, the primary form of religion throughout Mesopotamia was polytheism, and the gods were worshipped in the form of carved, molded, or sculpted idols. The center of each city-state boasted at least one tall religious tower—a ziggurat—where public religious observances were performed. In addition, most families had household altars adorned with cherished idols. When a king such as Nimrod was crowned, priests would invoke the blessings of the city's gods upon him and thereby establish the king's divine right to rule. The king, in turn, had an obligation to see that his subjects were faithful to the spiritual authority of the priests.[7]

The close alliance between religion and government was financed through a complex system of agricultural taxation. A certain portion of the crops of the area "belonged" to the gods, which meant that baskets of grain, onions, dates, and other goods were brought to the priests to be acknowledged, measured, and stored. A portion of the collected produce was then redistributed to feed religious or government workers and those who had fallen on hard times. Another portion was used to fund public works projects, such as repairing roads, renovating the king's palace, mending city walls, and keeping irrigation channels in good order.

When the system worked and the wealth was shared equitably, everyone flourished, the city stayed strong, and the kingship was stable. When war, famine, earthquakes, or other forces impaired the system, the resulting chaos could unseat the king and depose the priests. For Nimrod, the threat of being overtaken by a change in religion would have been as upsetting as hearing battering rams hit the gate of the city; surely nothing good could come of it.

HUNTING NIMROD

The story of Nimrod and his priests is filled with twists, turns, and surprises. The first big surprise is that Nimrod isn't at all who he seems to be. He couldn't possibly have been the ruler of Ur because he had already been dead for centuries by the time Abraham was born. What's more, the name *Nimrod* is nowhere to be found in the ancient lists of kings who ruled in various Mesopotamian cities during the time of Abraham. So why is he named as the king who "dreamed a dream?" Is scripture mistaken, or is there something lurking beneath the surface?

According to the Old Testament, the original Nimrod was a great-grandson of Noah and "a mighty hunter before the Lord." The reference to hunting sounds innocuous, but it isn't. It is an idomatic phrase filled with sinister undertones implying that Nimrod hunted men's souls in an effort to turn them away from God. But, like an appetizer, this tidbit of information is intriguing without being satisfying. To understand Nimrod at a deeper, more mystical level, to unearth his motivation for hunting souls, and to appreciate why, even though he was no longer alive, his name was invoked in connection with Abraham, it is necessary to open the Old Testament and examine a perplexing event in the life of Noah—the Prophet who was Nimrod's great-grandfather and also an ancestor of Abraham.

THE DRUNKENNESS OF NOAH

In the Book of Genesis, the drunkenness of Noah is described in these terms:

Noah, a man of the soil, was the first to plant a vineyard. He drank some of the wine and became drunk, and he lay uncovered in his tent. And Ham, the father of Canaan, saw the nakedness of his father, and told his two brothers outside. Then Shem and Japheth took a garment, laid it on both their shoulders, and walked backwards and covered the nakedness of their father; their faces were turned away, and they did not see their father's nakedness.

When Noah awoke from his wine and knew what his youngest son had done to him, he said, "Cursed be Canaan; lowest of slaves shall he be to his brothers." He also said, "Blessed by the Lord my God be Shem; and let Canaan be his slave. May God make space for Japheth, and let him live in the tents of Shem; and let Canaan be his slave."

After the flood Noah lived for three hundred and fifty years. All the days of Noah were nine hundred and fifty years; and he died.[8]

At first reading, this story comes across as crude, purposeless, and, with regard to periods of time, scientifically laughable. Moreover, Nimrod's name is never mentioned (and there seems to be no possible connection to Abraham). At second glance, when some of the underlying meanings are extracted and ancient idioms clarified, it stands revealed as a profound parable about the life-changing choices people make when confronted by a Prophet who reveals divine truths that are difficult to understand and accept. It also provides the origin of a religious disagreement divisive enough to produce shock waves that reverberated for centuries, eventually engulfing both Nimrod and Abraham.

In the last sentence of the story, Noah's "days" are given as nine hundred and fifty years, a life span that seems outrageously impossible and has occasioned many arguments among those who study the Bible. Thanks to recent discoveries by archaeologists, however, it is possible to understand the references to long life spans in a manner satisfactory to scientist and sage alike. The keys to understanding the long life spans lie in the hundreds of cuneiform tablets that have been excavated from ancient ruins. Four thousand years ago, these blocks of clay were the equivalent of paper. Scribes wrote on the wet clay with sharpened reeds, using a series of short, wedge-shaped strokes—called cuneiform—to create words. As soon as the clay was dry, a tablet could be taken home by the person who had commissioned it. Or, in the case of a king who had asked for a historical record of an event, the heavy tablet could be stored on sturdy shelves in the royal library.

In the process of translating and comparing some of the most recently excavated tablets, archaeologists have discovered that the reigns of many Mesopotamian kings are described in exactly the same way that the age of Noah is described: The kings are reported as having ruled for a far longer time than they actually did. No exact ratio has been determined, but it looks as though the higher the number, the more beloved or influential the ruler. Extending the reigns of some kings and omitting others was also a convenient way of summarizing history while retaining continuity.

Armed with this insight, it is easy to see that when the Book of Genesis says "all the days that Noah lived were nine hundred and fifty years," it is being neither scientifically inaccurate nor intentionally deceptive. Genesis is simply using the idiom of the time to condense several centuries of history into one easy phrase while simultaneously indicating Noah's long-lasting influence and the fact that His line continued through many generations of descendants. A similar use of language can be found in modern prose, such as an ad claiming "Silversmithing in the tradition of Paul Revere is alive and well today," although Paul himself died nearly two hundred years ago.[9]

Before unraveling the rest of the episode of Noah's drunkenness and clarifying its relationship to the lives of Nimrod and Abraham, it is necessary to acknowledge the deeply mystical nature of scripture. Warnings about its enigmatic symbolism are abundant but often underappreciated. A typical admonition is embedded in the Old Testament Book of Psalms, and, as the two versions below demonstrate, the translators themselves must have struggled with the challenge of faithfully conveying the meaning:

I will open my mouth in a parable:
I will utter enigmas from ancient time.[10]

I will open my mouth in a parable:
I will utter dark sayings of old.[11]

Moving forward in time and shifting to the New Testament, one finds Jesus doing the same thing: imparting spiritual knowledge in parables because this is "as much as they could understand." Six hundred years after Jesus, Muḥammad reiterated the idea that God "speaketh to mankind in allegories" that are difficult to penetrate. Twelve hundred years later, in 1862, Bahá'u'lláh praised the Word of God as being "an ocean inexhaustible in riches."[12]

Elucidating every particle of meaning in the episode of Noah's drunkenness is not within the capabilities of this author, but the three biblical verses below give clear hints about what type of vineyard Noah actually planted and what kind of wine He drank:

For the vineyard of the LORD of hosts
is the house of Israel . . .[13]

I am the true vine, and my Father is the husbandman.[14]

Thou hast showed thy people hard things:
thou hast made us to drink the wine of astonishment.[15]

Applying the allegorical meaning of these verses to the story of Noah elevates His actions to a realm far removed from physical vines and alcoholic beverages. He is not falling into a drunken stupor but is "intoxicated with the wine of the All-Merciful" and "carried away with the inebriating effect of the living waters of His loving providence."[16] Noah's mission is not to harvest a few grapes but to be a very special kind of gardener—a husbandman who obeys the word of the Father by sowing seeds of divine knowledge that will mature into the house of Israel. Abraham will spring from that vineyard, and His descendants will produce several other Messengers of God, each one a "true vine."

Reading further into the story of Noah, one finds Him "uncovered within his tent." Somewhat surprisingly, the state of being naked in order to receive new clothes is not especially unusual in scripture:

Naked am I, O my God!
Clothe me with the robe of Thy tender mercies.[17]

Now we know that if the earthly tent we live in is destroyed,
we have a building from God,
an eternal house in heaven, not built by human hands.
Meanwhile we groan,
longing to be clothed with our heavenly dwelling,
because when we are clothed, we will not be found naked.[18]

Noah is not physically nude but has stripped Himself of earthly desires and stands spiritually naked before God, ready to be clothed with the gift of heavenly understanding. Two of Noah's sons—Shem and Japheth—appreciate what is happening. They approach their father with reverence and cover Him with a fresh garment—the garment of their respect. In return, Noah promises blessings to their descendants. One of these blessings will be Abraham, who will be born from the line of Shem.

Noah's other son, Ham, is appalled by what his father is doing. He does not understand that Noah has drunk the wine of a new revelation from God. And he rejects the notion that Noah has been commanded to strip off His old clothes—His old traditions—in order to embark on a spiritual mission requiring different attitudes and behavior. Ham wants everything to stay as it is.

Ham's rejection of his father's astonishing wine and heavenly clothing is continued by two of Ham's descendants: a son named Canaan and a grandson called (aha!) Nimrod.

Canaan settles near the eastern shore of the Mediterranean Sea and establishes a thriving tribe. His descendants become known as Canaanites, and the territory they inhabit becomes the Land of Canaan. Later on, in an act of beautifully-orchestrated mystical irony, this spiritually bereft land is precisely where God will send Abraham.

Ham's grandson Nimrod grows up to become a ruler so cruel and ungodly that his name quickly degenerates into an epithet for anyone who is cruel, calculating, and unholy. When, generations later, the king who dreams about the birth of Abraham is referred to as a *Nimrod*, everyone who hears the tale knows immediately that he is the embodiment of iniquity. And they realize he will reject Abraham in the same way Ham rejected Noah. The king's real name doesn't matter at all.

2

A RISING STAR

Can you lead forth the constellations in their season?
Job[1]

During the years before Abraham's birth, the local ruler (who, because of his unspiritual nature, is referred to as Nimrod even though that was almost certainly not his given name) had a dream. The scripture continues, "Thereupon, he summoned the soothsayers, who informed him of the rise of a star in the heaven."[2] Although it seems clear that one meaning of this passage is symbolic—a brilliant Prophet will ascend and shine in the firmament of faith, swallowing up the religions of the past—there was also something very special and completely literal happening in the sky above Nimrod's head. Something that the soothsayers would have been aware of and perhaps worried about: the Age of Taurus was giving way to the Age of Aries.

An astronomical "age" is a period of about two thousand years during which a particular constellation is the dominant one in the sky of the northern hemisphere on the night of the spring equinox. These ages don't have exact beginnings and endings because the transition between them, when two constellations share the limelight, lasts at least a century. During the age of Taurus, the constellation of the Bull reigned, but in the years prior to Abraham,

Aries—the Ram—was moving in to displace it. The fact that this change would have been noticed and discussed by king, priest, and commoner alike can be traced to the influence of three of Abraham's prophetic ancestors: Adam, Seth, and Enoch.

Although Enoch was born several generations after Adam and Seth, all three of them lived in preliterate societies (roughly 4000 BC) when people were only just beginning to experiment with incising a few symbols on slabs of wet clay. Faced with the challenge of providing an easy-to-access source of inspiration, the three of them are credited with sketching imaginary lines among groups of stars and using the resulting images as giant illustrations for a celestial storybook of moral education. Along with the educational parables, they prophesied ways in which certain astronomical events in the future would be tied to the advent of other divine Messengers.[3]

It is not possible to reconstruct all of what was taught by this trio of prophets. Nor is anyone sure of the original names of the constellations or of all the ideas and virtues associated with them. Still, it is easy to imagine how enthralling it must have been for their followers to be able to lift their eyes to the sky and find spiritual sustenance in the twinkling tableaus above. These ancient viewers might not have been ready to understand monotheism, but they certainly could grasp the importance of the struggle between good and evil as demonstrated by Leo's efforts to subdue the untrustworthy serpent, Hydra, beneath his shaggy paw. They could also appreciate the generosity with which Aquarius poured water for the thirsty and anticipate how it might feel to have the worth of their own deeds weighed on the spiritual scales of Libra.

When it came to using the constellations as a clock, religious scholars such as Frances Rolleston have posited that Adam, Seth, and / or Enoch left prophecies about momentous events connected to a time when Taurus the Bull would be replaced by Aries the Ram and, after that, when the Ram would give way to the fishes of Pisces.[4] They might even have left hints about our own modern age, the Age of Aquarius, a time when the fishes yield to the water-bearer. These prophecies would have given a great boost to the science of astronomy by inspiring sky-watchers to investigate, record, and learn how to predict the movements of both fixed and wandering stars (planets were thought to be stars that moved in unexpected directions).

Centuries of practice in watching the sky for indications of important spiritual events would have given the royal soothsayers of Mesopotamia a reason to link Nimrod's dream to the way in which Aries was pushing Taurus out of the way. They would have been even more certain of their interpretation if, as is possible, an unusual planetary conjunction had taken place or a comet had floated through the constellation of Aries.

ABRAHAM IS BORN

While Nimrod paced back and forth, pondering the best method of eliminating the Prophet whose advent was predicted by his dream and the rising star, Abraham's mother, Emtelai, must have been equally worried about what the future held in store.[5] Knowing how frequently young women died in childbirth, she would have had reason to fear that she might not live to see the face of her child. When she went into labor, one of the household servants would have run to fetch a midwife while another relayed the news to the father-to-be.

The father-to-be, Emtelai's husband, was Terah (spelled in the Qur'án as *Azar*). He is thought to have been an educated and influential man who made a living manufacturing and selling idols. Often whitewashed with lime or painted with red and black pigments, the figurines of that era ranged in height from a few inches to a foot or more. Purchasers set them in the doorway of a house or business, placed them near a personal altar, or buried them under the threshold to protect the inhabitants against demons and other evil spirits. The idols were also worshiped in private family chapels, placed in curbside shrines, and entombed with the dead bodies of family members who lay moldering in a vault dug underneath the foundation of the house—a practice that could permeate the dwelling, or even the neighborhood, with a distinctly unpleasant odor.

One hopes that on the day Abraham was born, his mother's nose was filled with a more pleasant scent than that of rotting flesh. Perhaps barley bread topped with sesame seeds was baking in the kitchen oven, or maybe Emtelai was able to dab fragrant oil on her wrists. The midwife could have helped the labor along by giving Emtelai a medicinal wad of tree bark to chew or spreading ointment on her stomach and massaging it gently.

Terah's other wives—tradition counts two of them—might have waited nearby, perched on stools with woven reed seats, jingling their dainty ankle bracelets and sipping a lightly alcoholic beer brewed from dates. They could have helped Emtelai sit on a birthing stool and would have stretched out willing hands to hold the newborn, wipe him clean, and wrap him in a blanket woven of linen or wool.[6]

A naming ceremony was typically held a few days after the birth of a child, once it was clear the baby was healthy and likely to survive. Terah called his new son *Abram*, which means *exalted father* or *father lifted up*. In the future, as part of a special covenant, God would elongate Abram's name to *Abraham*—which, for the sake of simplicity, is what we will continue to call Him.

Children were important in Mesopotamia, but because it was a patriarchal society, sons were more important than daughters. Sons were the children who would continue the family business, support their parents in old age, bury them respectfully when the time came, and claim the largest share of the inheritance. The only thing better than birthing one son was having several, a feat Emetlai accomplished by producing two brothers for Abraham: Nahor, whose name means *light,* and then Haran, whose name is thought to refer to the town where either Terah or his father had been born.

The brothers were probably spaced two or three years apart, which was the customary period of time for a mother to continue breastfeeding (a practice that acts as a natural contraceptive). As the boys grew, learning to weave their way through narrow streets, they might have taken time to watch new houses being built. The materials were readily available—clay mixed with straw, molded into bricks, and dried in the hot sun of the early summer months when no rain was expected. The bricks were mortared together with tarry bitumen stiffened by the addition of sandy soil. Wood was used to outline doors and windows, though windows were few and most of the indoor illumination was provided by oil lamps. Roofs were made of palm tree planks covered with reeds and slathered with clay. The homes of the wealthy were built around a central courtyard and featured several bedrooms plus a kitchen with a pantry, a dining area, a place to bathe, and even a toilet suspended above a pit that drained into a central sewer through underground channels.[7]

Abraham, Nahor, and Haran might also have passed many childhood hours doing what all little boys do—driving their parents crazy by emulating the antics of local wrestlers, pounding on small drums, or pleading for yet another turn at a popular board game reminiscent of backgammon. The boys probably received a little schooling, at least enough to learn how to record basic business transactions in cuneiform characters on clay tablets. And, as heirs to the family business, they would have also been expected to emulate their father by helping him with his business of making and selling idols.

The idols of that period were human figures or fantastic animals sculpted from stone, carved from wood, cast in metal, or made of clay. Terah, working in wood and stone, was respected as a masterful craftsman who could turn out several beautiful idols in a single day.[8] As Abraham assisted His father, learning how to wield a hammer and chisel and finding out how to lure customers into the family's store, one of the things He discovered is as true now as it was then: handmade gods and goddesses are easily broken.

Jewish tradition describes Abraham's eye-opening experience of breakage as happening when Terah sent Abraham to sell idols in the streets of the city. The boy loaded the family mule with idols and headed for an inn where a group of Syrian merchants was staying. He hoped they would be interested in buying the idols for resale in Egypt. Just as Abraham reached the inn, a camel belched loudly enough to frighten the mule, which broke away and ran off.

In the resulting tumult, three valuable idols were broken, ruining Abraham's chance to make a profit and impress His father with His business acumen.

After the mule had been recaptured, Abraham straddled it and began riding home, reflecting as He rode on how totally helpless the idols had been. Ironically, Abraham's father, Terah, was more powerful than the gods he created. "Is not he the god of his gods," Abraham asked Himself, "for do they not come into being by reason of his carving and chiseling and contriving?"[9]

Whether the incident of the belching camel and the runaway mule was the catalyst or not, both tradition and scripture indicate that Abraham began asking penetrating questions about spiritual reality while still quite young. He was, according to the Bahá'í writings, a member of the Sabean Faith (see Appendix B), but the answers He found within that faith evidently didn't satisfy Him. As soon as He began drawing independent conclusions about the nature of reality, He began acting in ways that surprised His comrades, infuriated His father, and ultimately transformed Him into the rising star feared by Nimrod.

3

INTO THE FIRE

O the misery of men!
No Messenger cometh unto them but they laugh Him to scorn.
Muḥammad[1]

As soon as the young Abraham became convinced that idols have no power, He began sharing that realization with His father. When Terah turned away, refusing to listen to His arguments, Abraham adopted a more dramatic form of persuasion.

One day Terah was called away on business, and Abraham was left to mind the store. While He was on duty, a pious woman dropped by. She was carrying a handful of flour as an offering for the idols, and she spread it out in front of them so that they might eat it. Abraham responded courteously to the generosity of the woman and managed to refrain from pointing out the foolishness of her actions, but after she left, He grabbed a hammer and began energetically swinging it. With a blow here and a blow there, He managed to smash all of the idols, except one, to bits. He left the largest idol intact and put the hammer in its hand.

When Terah returned and discovered the damage, he was livid. What was the name, he demanded, of the madman who had ransacked the store? Abraham responded that a woman had come in with an offering of flour, and that when the gift was set in front of the idols, they started arguing. The greediest god irritated the others by announcing, "I will eat first." This caused a second god to protest, saying, "No, I will eat first!" The disagreement escalated until the biggest of them all stood up, grabbed a hammer and crushed the others to dust.

Terah stared at his son in disbelief. "Are you trying to fool me?" he asked. "These idols don't know anything."

Abraham quietly replied, "Do your ears not hear what your mouth has just said?"

Terah refused to be impressed by this performance, but Abraham remained adamant in His beliefs. Eventually He began speaking about His beliefs to people outside the family, directing them to abandon idols, renounce polytheism, and "Serve the God of all gods, the Lord of lords, who hath created heaven and earth, the sea and all therein."[2]

FROM POLYTHEISM TO MONOTHEISM

Abraham's vibrant rejection of polytheism and idol worship startled those around Him in spite of the fact that His ideas rested on a spiritual foundation built by the Prophets who preceded Him. Step by step, Adam, Seth, Enoch, Noah, and others had led mankind along a divine path that was intended to gradually move people away from worshipping the visible and limited and lead them toward an appreciation of the unseen and unlimited. These Messengers had emphasized basic moral concepts and explained the difference between good and evil. They had also established the existence of a god who was greater than any of the others, and he had been adopted by many cultures under a variety of names, including El, An, Il, and Horus.*

One thing that previous Messengers had not yet done (as far as can be determined) was to proclaim an end to polytheism and introduce monotheism. Nor, it seems, had they forbidden idols.

---

* A more complete discussion of names is contained in Chapter 7 of this book.

This was not a careless oversight on their part but a necessary strategy based on the spiritual capabilities of human beings. The Bahá'í writings explain that

> Just as the organic evolution of mankind has been slow and gradual, and involved successively the unification of the family, the tribe, the city-state, and the nation, so has the light vouchsafed by the Revelation of God, at various stages in the evolution of religion, and reflected in the successive Dispensations of the past, been slow and progressive. Indeed the measure of Divine Revelation, in every age, has been adapted to, and commensurate with, the degree of social progress achieved in that age by a constantly evolving humanity.[3]

Abraham's gigantic task would be to explain that the high god was the only god and that it was impossible to contain him in an idol or accurately represent him with a graven image. In pursuit of this goal, Abraham would find, as did others before and after Him, that the mantle of prophethood does not rest lightly on the shoulders of those who must bear it. Opposition and persecution, along with ridicule and contempt, are constant companions.

TRIAL BY FIRE

By the time Abraham started preaching, religious institutions scattered across the Middle East had lost most of the spirituality that originally inspired them and had become rigid, priest-controlled cults more concerned with maintaining power than investigating truth. When Abraham's words, like arrows, thudded against their walls of inflexible belief, the initial reaction of priest and commoner alike seems to have ranged from indifference to mild annoyance. No one took Him very seriously until, tradition recounts, an elderly woman responded to His ideas. She, astonishingly, "became a zealous missionary for the true God" and succeeded in converting others to this subversive point of view. News of the growing number of converts eventually reached the ears of the royal court, and the woman was summoned to appear before King Nimrod to explain herself.

As courageously as St. Catherine facing the Emperor of Rome or Ṭáhirih* calmly handing her own scarf to those who would strangle her, the woman explained her newfound belief. The king, furious at this affront to his own sovereignty, and maybe still worried about the threat of the rising star, "rebuked her harshly, asking her how she dared serve any god but himself." Her audacious reply—that there is only one true God—earned her a sentence of death.[4]

Rather than discouraging new converts, the martyrdom of this heroic woman—whose name we do not know—sparked a greater surge of interest, with predictable but unfortunate results. Abraham was summoned to meet with Nimrod and his priests. They commanded Him to acknowledge the gods of nature by bowing down before them, but Abraham refused, countering their demands with questions and arguments demonstrating the uselessness of worshipping inanimate objects. Several versions of the scene are available in Jewish tradition, and the conversation went something like this:

> "I command you to bow down to fire!"
> "Why not worship water that can extinguish the fire?"
> "Then bow to water."
> "Perhaps it would be better to worship the clouds that carry water as rain?"
> "Very well. Bow down to the clouds."
> "But wind is more powerful. It scatters the clouds."
> "Fine. Bow down to the wind."
> "Perhaps it would be better to worship a person who can endure the wind?"

---

* A devoted follower of the Báb who was martyred for her outspoken teaching of His message.

Nimrod, bewildered by Abraham's arguments and angered at His obstinacy, abruptly closed the interview with a horrifying judgment. "You speak nothing but meaningless words! I myself bow down only to fire. So now, behold, I will cast you into the midst of fire. Let your God rescue you if He can."[5]

The image of being cast into a fire foreshadows how King Nebuchadnezzar would someday deal with Shadrach, Meshach, and Abednego. It also invites a very pointed question: Just what kind of fire was it?

One of the oldest answers, given by Jewish rabbis pondering the lives of the Prophets, depicts Abraham being cast into a physical fire. The fire roared at the bottom of an earthen pit, ready to receive pieces of limestone which, when burned, would produce calcium oxide, an essential ingredient in the making of glass. As soon as Abraham was lowered into the fire, He felt the full agony of the thousand-degree temperature—but only for a moment, just enough to demonstrate His faith. The Angel Gabriel immediately flew to God and vehemently protested the burning of this innocent man. When God agreed to allow Gabriel to intervene, the angel shielded Abraham and carried Him out of the flames unscathed.

In another version of the story, Abraham's descent into the pit caused the logs of the fire to come alive and produce a flush of fresh buds. Green twigs unfurled from the buds, grew into sturdy limbs, and matured with supernatural rapidity into lush trees whose branches were laden with delicious fruits. The miracle transformed the pit into an exquisite garden, and Abraham's life was saved.

Muḥammad affirms the general story of trial by fire but doesn't explain the substance of the flames: "Said they, 'Build for him a pyre, and throw him into the flaming hell!' . . . We said, 'O fire! be thou cool and a safety for Abraham!'"[6]

Bahá'í scripture agrees that Abraham was thrown into a fire but makes it clear that the flames did not spring from wooden logs:

It is well known what a host of enemies besieged Him, until at last the fires of envy and rebellion were kindled against Him.[7]

And remember when Nimrod kindled the fire of polytheism whereby He would burn the Friend of God [Abraham]. Verily, we extinguished the fire by the truth and brought upon Nimrod manifest grief.[8]

The image of a fire extinguisher filled with truth quenching the flames of polytheism, envy, and rebellion is a potent one. It shoots us straight into the heart of a spiritual revolution created by a young man who was "an iconoclast and a Herald of the oneness of God."[9]

Abraham's reward for telling the truth, smashing idols, and withstanding the flames of polytheism was not acclaim, riches, or even a single small compliment. Instead, Nimrod and his priests expelled Abraham, sending Him five hundred miles away into what is now southern Turkey but was then the wild'n'woolly northern frontier of the Mesopotamian Empire.

The reason why Abraham was exiled rather than being executed for His heresy may have lain in His father's popularity as a maker of gods. If Nimrod feared Terah's influence over the gods he created at work each day, the king would have been wary of the consequences of enraging Terah by killing his firstborn son. Possibly he had come to fear that Abraham, too, was capable of influencing these gods. And, to top it all off, there was the nagging question of how Abraham's followers might behave if their leader were executed. Banishment to a place so remote that the banished would be forgotten must have seemed the wisest possible course of action.

4

EXILE

Every morning I waken to find
that I am made a target for the darts of their envy,
and every night, when I lie down to rest,
I discover that I have fallen a victim to the spears of their hate.
Bahá'u'lláh[1]

Depending on the source, Abraham is considered to be a patriarch, a Messenger of God, a Prophet, or just a nice and very wise man. This book relies on the description of Abraham provided by the most recent of the five Abrahamic religions: the Bahá'í Faith.

Bahá'u'lláh, like Muḥammad before Him, refers to Abraham as a "Friend of God," a term indicating that Abraham was a divinely-inspired Manifestation. In Bahá'í terminology, a Manifestation of God is a Messenger created by God to transmit religious teachings to mankind. These Messengers embody the attributes of God, but They are not God descended to earth. They provide, rather, a perfect reflection of the divine attributes, in the same way that a mirror can provide a perfect reflection of the sun without actually being the sun.[2]

Manifestations of God are all inspired by the same Holy Spirit of God, and all of them receive divine knowledge about the past and future. In spite of what they have in common, however, the

Revelation imparted by each one is a little different than that of any of the others. The reason behind this individuality is that each Messenger shapes the way in which He imparts spiritual teachings, mystical wisdom, and social laws to suit the needs and circumstances of the age in which He lives. Among the Manifestations of God identified in Bahá'í scripture are Abraham, Krishna, Moses, Zoroaster, Buddha, Jesus, Muḥammad, the Báb, and Bahá'u'lláh.

No one knows exactly how old Abraham was when He realized that He was destined to be a Messenger of God, but a fair guess is that it occurred during His battles with the flames of polytheism in Ur, perhaps while He was in prison awaiting the sentence of exile. If so, His experience would have been akin to that of Bahá'u'lláh who, in 1850, received His divine summons while confined in a filthy underground cell in Tehran, His neck laden with over a hundred pounds of chain: "During the days I lay in the prison of Ṭihrán, though the galling weight of the chains and the stench-filled air allowed Me but little sleep, still in those infrequent moments of slumber I felt as if something flowed from the crown of My head over My breast, even as a mighty torrent that precipitateth itself upon the earth from the summit of a lofty mountain. Every limb of My body would, as a result, be set afire."[3]

The transforming experience, the moment in which the responsibility of being a divine herald was revealed to Abraham, is described in the Qur'án. In that verse, Muḥammad explains that Abraham was allowed to see beyond the physical limits of space and time so that He would have the information He needed to accomplish His mission: "Thus did We show Abraham the kingdom of the heavens and the earth that he might be of those possessing certainty."[4]

Was Abraham elated, terrified, saddened by what He learned? And how did He describe His encounter to others? Jewish tradition suggests that Abraham compared hearing the Word of God to eating nourishing food, and that the first person to hear the analogy was the warden of the prison. It seems that while Abraham was in prison He was fed very little if any food, in the hope that He would starve to death. When an order finally came to release Abraham from His cell, a warden approached warily and called out "Abraham, art thou alive?"

Abraham answered, "I am living."

The warden, astonished, then asked, "Who has been bringing thee food and drink all these many days?"

Abraham replied, "Food and drink have been bestowed upon me by Him who is over all things, the God of all gods and the Lord of all lords, who alone doeth wonders, He who is the God of Nimrod and the God of Terah and the God of the whole world. He dispenseth food and drink unto all beings. He sees, but He cannot be seen, He is in the heavens above, and He is present in all places, for He Himself superviseth all things and provideth for all."[5]

FROM UR TO HARRAN

By the time Abraham was released from prison under the sentence of exile, He was old enough to have taken a wife, and so were His brothers. Haran, the youngest of the brothers, had already married and fathered three children—two girls, Milcah and Iscah, plus a boy named Lot. Then, as soon as Haran's daughter, Milcah, was old enough, Nahor (the middle brother) took her as his wife.

The woman who became Abraham's wife was named Sarai. After a few years, God would change her name to Sarah, which is the version that will be used throughout this book. According to the Bahá'í writings, Sarah was the sister (presumably the much younger sister) of Abraham's mother, which means that Abraham married His aunt.[6]

The marriages of Nahor to his niece and Abraham to His aunt sound incredibly incestuous to modern ears, but they were perfectly respectable in Ur of the Chaldees because the structure of society and its laws were different. As the Bahá'í writings explain, "During the time of the Abrahamic Prophethood it was considered allowable, because of a certain exigency, that a man should marry his aunt, even as Sarah was the sister of Abraham's mother. During the cycle of

Adam it was lawful and expedient for a man to marry his own sister, even as Abel, Cain and Seth, the sons of Adam, married their sisters. But in the law of the Pentateuch revealed by Moses these marriages were forbidden and their custom and sanction abrogated."[7]

Abraham's age on His wedding day isn't known, but using the description in Genesis of Sarah as ten years younger, a reasonable guess is that she was fifteen and He was twenty-five years old. Allowing for the time it took for the youngest brother, Haran, to grow up and then raise a daughter old enough for Nahor to marry, Abraham must have been about thirty-five years old when He angered King Nimrod and was ordered to leave Ur. By then, He and Sarah would have been married for ten years without conceiving any children, which meant that Sarah was considered by all to be hopelessly barren.

According to the Book of Genesis, three family members accompanied Abraham when He left Ur: His wife, Sarah; His father, Terah; and His nephew, Lot, who was the son of Haran. Haran himself, sadly, had no choice about whether or not to join the travelers because he was already dead. According to tradition, he loved his older brother but wasn't quite sure what to do when Abraham was cast into the flaming pit. Rather than leap in beside Him and share His fate, Haran stood aside, dithering. When the flames proved cool and Abraham unhurt, Haran finally jumped, but it was too late. The flames immediately blazed up and incinerated him.[8]

Having already pondered the nature of Nimrod's blaze, we are left to wonder about the circumstances of Haran's reported death. Was his soul consumed by envy, rebellion, and polytheism, making his death a spiritual one that rendered him of no further interest to religious history? Or was he physically dead as well? After four thousand years of uncertainty, the question still hasn't been answered.

As soon as the group of travelers had strapped carriers on the backs of donkeys, loaded a cart, and checked waterskins for holes, they would have begun their trek, striking out during cool, pre-dawn hours that would give way to a hot and dusty day. Alternatively, they might have packed bags to be loaded on camels while they themselves walked beside the plodding animals as part of a slow-moving caravan. If Sarah tired easily, she could have ridden at least part of the way in a cart pulled behind one of the camels. Although archaeologists doubt that camels were being bred and trained in Ur itself during Abraham's lifetime, the animals had already been domesticated in Arabia and are thought to have been used by at least a few Mesopotamian traders.[9]

A third travel possibility would have been a slow-moving boat that was partly sail-powered, partly towed with ropes held by strong men trudging along the riverbank, straining against the current. The boat would follow a longer and more twisting route than the road, but it was far less strenuous for the travelers.

As the exiles prepared to depart, they could look out from the high ground of the city and gaze over a green and fertile landscape created by the Euphrates. Rather than running neatly between parallel banks, the enormous river system branched and rebranched, forming a labyrinth made up of six thousand square miles of meandering creeks, shallow lakes, marshes, and islets.[10] Marsh dwellers wove floating houses out of pliant reeds and poled their way through the landscape in bitumen-tarred skiffs curved gracefully as crescent moons. They netted fish, took eggs from the nests of wild birds, and gathered other edibles.

Fanning out from the edge of the marsh were extensively irrigated fields that produced wheat, barley, onions, pomegranates, dates, and more. Nomads camped in seasonally green pastures near the river to fatten flocks of goats and sheep, whose wool, meat, milk, leather, and bone would be bartered for grain, spices, and other necessities.

The mosquito-plagued marshland could be roaringly dangerous during spring floods, fantastically hot and humid in summer, and treacherous in winter; but it was also lush and captivating. Blazing days melted into lavender evenings that were sometimes enlivened by the music of drums, cymbals, reed flutes, or lyres. It must have been agonizing for the exiles to accept that they could never return to "life in a land where great beds of huge, pale gold reeds reached up out of calm lakes; where nearly every villager held out a welcoming hand, where ducks and cormorants and herons rose in vast flocks to the skies . . ."[11]

A CIRCUITOUS ROUTE

According to scripture, the ultimate destination of Abraham— the arena of action to which He, the newest divine Messenger, was being called by God—was the Land of Canaan. When Abraham was banished, however, Nimrod didn't send Him westward to Canaan. Instead, he pointed to the north, to the belly of Turkey, and named the town of Harran as the place of exile.

A plausible line of thought suggests Harran was chosen not because Nimrod especially liked it but because Abraham's father, Terah, specifically requested it. The logic of this scenario rests on the notion that either Terah or his parents were natives of Harran. The evidence pointing most directly to this is the similarity of the name of Terah's youngest son, Haran, to the name of the town of Harran (indeed, many translations use the same spelling— *Haran*—for both names). If the reasoning is correct, the exiles might well have expected to receive help—shelter, food, and even a job—from their relatives.

Harran was situated in what is now southern Turkey, about twenty-five miles southeast of Urfa (usually listed on modern maps as *Sanliurfa*). It lay at the junction of several ancient trade routes, a fact reflected by the meaning of its name, generally translated as *crossroads* or *highway*. To get there from Ur, Abraham and His companions followed a well-established route running to the northwest, paralleling the Euphrates and skirting the edge of the enormous Syrian Desert. After a month or two, and a distance of four to five hundred miles at a presumed pace of ten to twenty miles a day, they entered a broad river valley where winters were mild and summers very hot "'with an abundance of gnats and lions.'"[12]

The buildings of Harran lay along the banks of the river Jullab, a spring-fed tributary of a larger river, the Balikh, which in turn ran into the Euphrates. Established by Ur as a merchant outpost, the village was occupied primarily by a confederation of seminomadic tribes who catered to the needs of traders from many lands, including Egypt, Oman, Syria, Iran, Iraq, Afghanistan, northern Turkey, and even the Indus valley (the land along the Indus River, which runs all the way through the middle of Pakistan before flowing into the Arabian Sea). Harran would later expand into a wealthy, cosmopolitan city, but when Abraham arrived, it seems to have been not much more than a small settlement.[13]

Once the family members had reached Harran, most of them must have sighed with relief. One can presume that Abraham, as a Messenger of God, saw dark clouds gathering on the horizon, but the others probably didn't realize that their true destiny lay in Canaan rather than in Harran. As they lay down to sleep each night, Sarah, Lot, and Terah probably thought the worst was over.

5

THREAT AND PROMISE

. . . and he died in Haran.
Genesis[1]

When Abraham, Sarah, Terah, and Lot reached Harran, they would have seen a cluster of houses constructed of sun-dried brick and shaped like old-fashioned beehives, a type of construction that had been popular for at least ten thousand years. The origin of the shape is credited to the volcanic eruption of Erciyes Dağı (Mt. Argaeus) in central Turkey sixty million years ago. Lava spread out and covered the land in a deep circle eighty miles wide. Wind and water gradually eroded the lava "but as always in nature, unevenly: hard basaltic rocks littering the valley floor protected the softer volcanic stone directly beneath, leaving conical pillars standing like sentinels as the surrounding plain weathered away. Early Anatolian man hollowed out the cones by patient chiseling with flint and copper tools, and they became snug and secure habitations . . ."[2]

Later generations copied the shape of the cones when building their own mud brick homes because the design was extremely practical for a desert climate. The conical roof shed rainwater in a flash, before it could seep into the bricks and soften them. The interior dome allowed hot air to rise away from the living area during the day, but at night the thick walls released the sun's stored heat and warmed those sleeping inside. Small homes would have just a single dome, but larger ones might have several, each with one or two rooms beneath it. While outdoor temperatures ranged from 60°F at night to 110°F or more at noon, the interior of a beehive house stayed at a comfortable 75°F–85°F.[3]

Although the town of Harran was not, in 2000 BC, the extensive and cosmopolitan city it would eventually become, its people were already deeply involved in worshipping a moon god who had the memorable name of *Sin*. The veneration of Sin was destined to continue for centuries, surviving the influences of succeeding waves of conquerors. Various groups of Mesopotamians—Akkadians, Babylonians, and Assyrians—took turns occupying the city until it passed into Persian rule when the Medes (Iranians) conquered the area in the sixth century BC. After that, control of the city bounced back and forth among the Persians, the Greeks, and the Romans.

The town's devotion to Sin remained and flourished from generation to generation and century to century, thanks in large part to the way that both priests and believers were willing to adopt new ideas and images from conquering rulers without actually converting. For instance, they adopted the goddess Ningal from Ur, but then they married her to Sin and put her in a separate temple. When the Zoroastrian Persians were in power, Sin's adherents accepted the idea of ethical dualism (the battle between good and evil) from Zoroastrianism and wove it into their own view of the cosmos. These stalwart worshippers may even have borrowed a few things from Hinduism, for old records indicated that the inhabitants of Harran somehow obtained an "Idol of the Water" from India and mounted it in a special temple to the east of the city.[4]

Christian missionaries made some converts among the citizens of Harran in the years following Jesus' death and constructed a sturdy basilica, but again, most of the local power continued to be held by priests at the temple of Sin. The greatest threat to the continuation of the cult of the moon god came in the ninth century AD when an invading Muslim army gave residents a choice of conversion or death. According to one account, the priests of Sin placated the invaders by appropriating for themselves the Qur'ánic label of *Sabians*,* mentioned by Muḥammad as acceptable believers in God, while simultaneously praying for the destruction of the mosque and continuing to worship Sin.

Harran's strength and religious dedication continued until AD 1000 or so, when the flow from underground aquifers lessened, probably due to increased irrigation of farms, orchards, and gardens in the broad Jullab-Balikh valley. After Mongol raiders sacked Harran in 1259, the upstream town of Urfa underwent a growth spurt and diverted ever greater amounts of the valley's water for its own use. In time, the Jullab River, on which Harran had depended, shriveled into an insignificant arroyo, flowing only during rainstorms, and the formerly sweet wells of the city of the moon god degenerated into brackish sinkholes. When Lawrence of Arabia visited the ruins of Harran in 1911, dining on cucumbers, bread, and mulberries with the local sheikh, the water he drank had to be hauled from a well that lay a mile away.[5]

The reliable well from which Lawrence's water came was named, according to his diary, after Rebekah, who lived in Harran as a girl and drew water from the well before moving to Canaan and marrying one of Abraham's sons. Bafflingly, forty years after Lawrence's visit, what had been *Rebekah's Well* was being referred to as *Jacob's Well (Bi'r Ya'qub)*, honoring Rebekah's son, Jacob, in spite of the fact that Jacob never lived in Harran.[6]

All in all, ancient Harran was not a town from which a reviled monotheistic Prophet could expect an enthusiastic welcome. Still, one gathers from tradition that Abraham and Sarah tried to make the best of their new environment. They raised flocks of sheep while living in a mud brick house situated on a gentle hill.[7]

Examination of excavated remains reveals that there were at least three distinct types of sheep that might have been found in Abraham's herd. One type had corkscrew horns, medium-length tails, and fairly smooth, hairy coats. A second strain sported short

---

* Also spelled *Sabeans*; see Appendix B for more information.

tails and Ammon horns (heavily ridged and curved into enormous spirals), and its fleece was very curly. The third kind of sheep had very long, fat tails with productive lanolin glands that made the long strands of its wool soft and silky.[8] Because fabric woven from woolen thread, hides with the fleece still attached, and panels of tanned leather were extensively used for clothing and for constructing household items, there was a widespread trade in freshly-shorn fleece as well as pelts. Goats, whose hides were also valuable, were often mixed into sheep herds, and the milk and meat from both types of animals were in constant demand.

At first, Abraham did not mention His beliefs to anyone. He maintained this silence until rumors about the way He had confronted Nimrod reached the ears of local Harranians. The rumors aroused so much curiosity that the townspeople began seeking Him out to ask questions. Then and only then did Abraham break His silence and try to convey the truth of monotheism to them. In deference to the customs of the time, Abraham spoke only to men, while Sarah accepted the responsibility of speaking with any of the women who wanted to learn more.[9]

The general reaction to Abraham's teachings was negative. "These people believed not in one God but in many gods, to whom they ascribed miracles," the Bahá'í writings explain, "therefore, they all arose against Him, and no one supported Him except Lot, His brother's son, and one or two other people of no importance."[10] Abraham's father, Terah, joined the adamant opposition, which indicates that he had continued to cling to his profession of making and selling idols.

Muḥammad describes Abraham's anguished attempts to reason with His father and persuade him to accept a new divine Message this way: "O my Father! why dost thou worship that which neither seeth nor heareth, nor profiteth thee aught? . . . verily now hath knowledge come to me which hath not come to thee. Follow me therefore—I will guide thee into an even path." To clinch the argument, Abraham added a warning to his pleas: "worship not Satan, for Satan is a rebel against the God of Mercy . . . indeed I fear lest a chastisement from the God of Mercy light upon thee, and thou become Satan's vassal."[11]

Terah, unwilling to abandon earthbound images, responded to Abraham's arguments with ferocious rejection, sundering the family bonds that had united them during the exile from Ur. "Castest thou off my gods, O Abraham?" he demanded. "If thou forbear not, I will surely stone thee. Begone from me for a length of time."[12]

When someone adamantly opposes God (becomes a "companion of the Fire"), Muḥammad says it not fitting for a Prophet to pray for his forgiveness, even if he is a close relative. Nevertheless, Abraham responded to His father's threats of banishment and stoning in the same tenderhearted way that Jesus asked forgiveness for those who crucified Him. "Peace be on thee!" exclaimed Abraham. "I will pray my Lord for thy forgiveness, for he is gracious to me."[13]

In His prayer, Abraham begged God not to let Him become a test or a trial to any person who, like His father, disbelieved. Only when it was abundantly clear that Terah was determined to remain an enemy did Abraham agree to ". . . separate myself from you, and the gods ye call on besides God." And then, having been mercilessly cut loose from the normal duties of an eldest son toward his father, Abraham turned to the source of divine mercy, saying "on my Lord will I call."[14]

God's answer to Abraham's call came in the form of a magnificent promise:

> Leave your country and your people and your father's household
> and go to the land I will show you.
> I will make you into a great nation and I will bless you;
> I will make your name great, and you will be a blessing.
> I will bless those who bless you,
> and whoever curses you I will curse;
> and all peoples on earth will be blessed through you.[15]

In lively minds, being cursed by God stirs up visions of a vengeful finger shooting bolts of lightning at the miscreant. Scripture, by contrast, holds a different, more metaphysical point of view in which the state of being cursed or blessed is explained in terms of natural consequences. It is analogous to the way that being burned by a hot stove is a natural consequence of touching it and not the result of active persecution by the stove. From this point of view, the laws of God's universe include scientific realities like the speed of light or the effect of gravity as well as moral realities like honesty and love. As mentioned in the gospel of Matthew, breaking or ignoring any of these fundamental laws is a spiritually dangerous enterprise:

> Everyone who hears these words of Mine
> And does not act on them
> Will be like a foolish man who built his house on the sand.
> The rain fell, and the floods came,
> and the winds blew and slammed against that house;
> and it fell—and great was its fall.[16]

Or, as Job puts it, "they that plow iniquity, and sow wickedness, reap the same."[17]

By refusing to acknowledge the truth when he heard it and, even worse, threatening the life of a Messenger of God, Terah voluntarily moved away from the state of being blessed (accepting and rejoicing in the love of God) and joined the ranks of those who wished to live in the state of being cursed (refusing and abhorring the love of God). "Love Me, that I may love thee," Bahá'u'lláh says, because "If thou lovest Me not, My love can in no wise reach thee."[18]

Just as Nimrod's name became a synonym for a dolt or a fool, Terah's name continued to be so strongly identified with spiritual aridity that it has been used as a metaphor for the difficulties Moses faced in trying to teach the Israelites about God: "Moses lived in the wilderness of Terah."[19]

Genesis indicates that Terah died before Abraham left Harran. But, as was the case with the prior "death" of Abraham's brother, Haran, the Old Testament may not be speaking of physical demise but, instead, conveying a mystical truth. When Terah threatened to stone his son and thereby kill a Messenger of God, he was committing spiritual suicide. Though alive and breathing the air of this planet, he was lifeless enough to merit being grouped with those of whom Jesus said, "Let the dead bury their dead."[20]

Like Moses leaving Egypt or the Báb shivering in an icy prison cell,* Abraham had already faced years of opposition in His attempt to introduce a new Revelation. And now, having survived the flames of polytheism, the judgment of Nimrod, and the exile to Harran, there was more to come. This second banishment would push Abraham completely beyond the bounds of Mesopotamia and into an alien culture where, His enemies hoped, "He might be crushed and destroyed . . . that no trace of Him might be left."[21]

---

* After declaring His mission, the Báb was imprisoned in the fortress of Máh-Kú, a town in present-day Iran, where the water with which He washed was "of such icy coldness that its drops glistened as they froze upon His face" (Nabíl-i-A'ẓam, *The Dawn-Breakers: Nabíl's Narrative of the Early Days of the Bahá'í Revelation*, p. 252).

6

ON THE ROAD AGAIN

*History warns us
that it is the customary fate of new truths
to begin as heresies.*
Thomas Huxley[1]

At the moment when Abraham agreed to placate His father by leaving Harran and accepting God's call to "go to the land I will show you," His physical circumstances were bleak. His foes had every reason to believe that in the very near future both Abraham and His monotheistic message would disappear.

Inwardly, however, in the world of spiritual reality, the situation was quite the opposite. When a divine Messenger like Abraham refuses to recant and willingly accepts the sufferings imposed on Him, His actions have profound repercussions for succeeding generations:

> Abraham's migration from His native land caused the bountiful gifts of the All-Glorious to be made manifest . . . The flight of Moses, the Prophet of Sinai, revealed the Flame of the Lord's burning Fire, and the rise of Jesus breathed the breaths of the Holy Spirit into the world. The departure of Muḥammad, the Beloved of God, from the city of His birth was the cause of the exaltation of God's Holy

Word, and the banishment of the Sacred Beauty [Bahá'u'lláh] led to the diffusion of the light of His divine Revelation throughout all regions.[2]

Still, no matter how clearly Abraham understood the eventual spiritual outcome of this second banishment, no matter how comprehensively He explained it to Sarah, the thought of spending the rest of their lives in exile had to be daunting. Harran, the site of their first exile, might be a frontier town in comparison to Ur, but it held members of the tribe to which they belonged, and its culture was at least slightly familiar. Canaan, the land to which God was sending them, was completely outside of the bounds of Mesopotamia. They would be forced to find a way to establish a household in an alien environment and make a living among potentially hostile people who spoke a different language.

As far as can be determined, Abraham and Sarah didn't have very much in the way of personal possessions to take with them into exile. Perhaps they managed to trade the house and the livestock they are thought to have had while in Harran for portable wealth in the form of pieces of silver. They might even have begun the final exile in classic nomadic fashion, herding before them a flock of sheep and goats from which to take sustenance—or barter for supplies—as they moved along.

After Terah's death—whether physical or spiritual—Abraham's nephew, Lot, was the only family member left who was willing to undertake the perilous journey with Abraham and Sarah. The rest of the travel party is described in Genesis as "the people they had got" while in Harran. We don't know whether these people were servants, adventurers, or converts—or a combination of all three—but the phrase "people they had got" may indicate that some members of the group were there because they had been attracted by Abraham's teachings. This interpretation stems from the Rabbinic understanding that when a man teaches someone about God—"gets" him for God—it is as though he personally has made or begotten that person. The same understanding of being born or made exists in Christianity, as when the New Testament mentions that "Jesus made and baptized more disciples than John." It also appears in the Bahá'í Faith when those who teach others about the new religion are referred to as "spiritual parents."[3]

COUNTING BIRTHDAYS

In the Old Testament, Abraham is described as being seventy-five years of age when He left Harran, a statement that produces a mental image of a white-haired patriarch leaning on a staff and hobbling out of town. In absolute solar years, however, Abraham was probably about forty—no longer young but certainly not a card-carrying senior. The seeming conflict between what is physically likely and what is written in scripture cannot be understood without delving into the meanings of ancient idioms. These figures of speech were perfectly clear to Moses, the Messenger of God who, in approximately 1350 BC, summed up spiritual history in a form that could be digested and remembered by His followers. The idioms were also clear to the Israelites who began making the first written records of what Moses had revealed in the eighth century BC, thereby creating the five books of the Old Testament, often referred to as the *Torah*: Genesis, Exodus, Leviticus, Numbers, and Deuteronomy.

As mentioned in chapter 1, researchers studying cuneiform tablets have discovered that many of the previous civilizations of the Middle East felt no obligation to submit an accurate count of solar years when describing important events, preferring to record blocks of time in ways that were deemed auspicious or satisfied a love of mathematical symmetry. This led to tablets that cited the reigns of various kings as having lasted a hundred years or more, even if the king died young.[4]

These same civilizations also had little or no interest in establishing anyone's true chronological age. Instead, they used a few specific numbers to indicate general stages of life, though it isn't clear exactly how or why these were chosen. In the same way we casually refer to someone as a teenager or a young adult, they might describe him as being forty years old. When that person reached the stage of marrying and raising children, he or she would be depicted as being fifty or sixty. The age of ninety was reserved for those who were considered extremely long-lived: approximately sixty to seventy solar years. Even the age of one's death was flexible. Someone who died at the ripe age of forty or fifty solar years—or even at eighty—would be touted as having died at exactly one hundred and twenty. An even more extreme number—the astounding sum of three thousand six hundred years—was used when one wanted to extend sincere wishes for a lengthy life; it took that long, it was said, to see strands of gray appear in the dark beard of a grandson.[5]

So there it is, an answer to the puzzle. When Abraham is mentioned in Genesis as being seventy-five years old, it's not a deception, an exaggeration, or a mistake. It's also not the number of candles on His birthday cake. The idiom is simply conveying the information that Abraham isn't a child or teenager anymore. He's somewhat past the age when a man might be expected to have a child or two, but He's still solidly in the middle of adulthood.

With all these patterns in mind, it's easy to appreciate how deftly Moses used numerical idioms. By describing Adam, Noah, and many of His other predecessors as having lived for extraordinary periods of time, Moses was able to skip lightly across a wide expanse of time and compress centuries of spiritual history into a numinous narrative that indicated the general flow of genealogy, outlined the continuing chain of religious responsibility, and spoke prophetically of the future.

Between the death of Moses and the birth of Jesus, there were extraordinary changes in language, culture, and the ways in which people counted minutes, hours, days, and years. The numerical idioms of previous eras were gradually abandoned and forgotten, a loss that caused great confusion in succeeding centuries and, for many people, drove a bitter wedge between science and religion. Modern scholars who have unearthed the evidence necessary to resolve this quandary deserve a round of applause.

Four thousand years ago, the death rate of infants and children was very high, but it was possible for a healthy adult to live into his fifties and, beyond that, even into his eighties or nineties. So when Abraham set out for Canaan, most likely at the age of forty, His body was still in the prime of its life. Stretching out in front of Him were several decades in which He could continue to spread the new Revelation from God. His period of ministry would be much longer, certainly, than that of the Báb, who had just six years to spread His Revelation before being martyred at the age of thirty. It would be longer, too, than that of Jesus, who also met an early death. And it would exceed the nineteen years Muḥammad had between the public announcement of His mission in AD 613 and His death in AD 632.

THE ROUTE TO CANAAN

The primary route from Harran to Canaan, the one Abraham is most likely to have trod, was nothing close to a straight line. The road began in southern Turkey, stretched into western Syria, and then meandered along a zigzagging course to the south through the heart of Lebanon and into Canaan / Israel.* The primary reason for the wiggly route was water. No savvy traveler—with or without accompanying animals—dared venture across arid distances without being certain he could replenish his supply of this precious liquid at predictable intervals.

The first fifty miles of the road moved across a series of springs and brooks where one could rest in the heat of midday or set up a camp at night. At the first major river—the Orontes—the route turned south, following the waterway. In northern Lebanon, near the origin of the Orontes, the route switched to the banks of a second river—the Litani.

---

* Eager hikers who can't wait to lace up their boots and walk in Abraham's footsteps may want to follow the route developed by Abraham's Path (http://www. abrahampath.org). It covers more than three hundred (noncontiguous) miles of trail in Turkey, Jordan, the Palestinian Territories, and Israel.

The final leg of the trip ran beside a fresh and beautiful stream nourished by snowmelt from the high, cold mountains that stretch across the border between Israel and Lebanon. When the stream flowed into the Sea of Galilee (a freshwater lake in spite of its name), travelers could continue around the lake to its southern end, where the water exited, and follow the River Jordan into the center of Canaan.

Because of the numerous twists, turns, and ups and downs of the route, the number of miles Abraham, Sarah, and Lot would cover before reaching Canaan was at least twice the four hundred point-to-point miles a ruler would measure. Accompanied by a meandering flock of sheep and goats, the pace would have been quite slow. On days when it was necessary to stop before sunset in order to erect a tent in which to sleep, even fewer miles would have passed beneath their feet. If they traveled more lightly, using pieces of silver as their means of exchange and riding at least part of the way in donkey-pulled carts or on an animal's back, the rate of progress would have been better, but the speediest journey of all—taking only a week or two—would have been by water.

The harbor nearest Harran was a hundred and fifty miles away on the eastern shore of the Mediterranean. After reaching it, the travelers could buy passage on a boat sailing and / or rowing its way down the coast. There were dozens of small waterfront villages dotting the long coast where the boats could stop to wait out a storm, pick up fresh food, and load or unload cargo. Depending on the weather, the journey could be completed in a week or two.

There are several places where Abraham, Sarah, and Lot could have ended their trip and stepped from the boat onto the soil of the land that would be their new home. One of the most likely choices would have been the port of Acre (also known as 'Akka or Akko). It is one of the oldest continuously inhabited cities in the world, and it is also the place where, four thousand years after Abraham, Bahá'u'lláh and His family disembarked in 1868.[6]

Although separated by nearly four thousand years, the parallels between the banishments suffered by Abraham and Bahá'u'lláh are striking. After first being exiled from Persia (modern-day Iran), Bahá'u'lláh lived for seven years in Baghdad, which lies well within the region once known as Ur of the Chaldees and is less than forty miles from Kutha, the town named by Jewish tradition as the birthplace of Abraham. Condemned as religious heretics, both Abraham and Bahá'u'lláh, as well as Their wives, were expelled from Iraq and forced to move to Turkey. After settling in Turkey, Abraham and Bahá'u'lláh were again harassed for Their beliefs. Both of Them, still accompanied by faithful wives, left Their homes again, destined to live out the rest of Their years in Canaan / Palestine / Israel. Today, Bahá'u'lláh's grave near Acre lies just a hundred miles away from the tomb of Abraham in Hebron.

7

THE LAND OF CANAAN

Never any weary traveler complained
that he came too soon to his journey's end.
Thomas Fuller[1]

By whatever route He finally chose, Abraham's preordained destination was a narrow strip of land known as Canaan. Hemmed in by desert to the east and the Mediterranean Sea to the west, Canaan covered an area that was longer, though not much wider, than the current boundaries of Israel.

The northern edge of Canaan extended up into Syria, encompassing what today is Lebanon. Its southern end spilled out into a triangular peninsula that resembled a canine tooth, hence the name on today's maps—*Sinai*—which means *teeth* in Arabic. The wide northern coast of the Sinai Peninsula, washed by the waters of the Mediterranean Sea, created the top of the tooth. Its tapering sides, embraced by the Gulf of Aqaba and the Gulf of Suez—led to a sharp southern tip that dipped into the Red Sea.

The Sinai Peninsula was the only land bridge connecting Eurasia and Africa, making it one of the most strategically important pieces of property in the world. Canaan, right next door, was forced into becoming the country through which every intercontinental caravan had to pass in order to reach its ultimate destination. But, in spite of the potential profit to be made by anyone living along a popular trade route, Canaan was a challenging place in which to settle because it was so often disrupted by war when neighboring superpowers invaded in order to gain control over its convenient harbors and inland pathways. And even in years when peace reigned, Canaan was often besieged by the vagaries of an unreliable climate.

In the spring and summer, desiccating desert wind hissed across Canaan's sunburned hills for months at a time, sucking moisture from everything in its path. When the wind finally changed and winter clouds tumbled in from the ocean, laden with vital rain, the ferocity of the resulting storms often flattened cool-season crops, eroded hills, and flooded valleys. Earthquakes produced by numerous geological faults were not uncommon, and a severe jolt could shake a village to bits in less than sixty seconds.[2]

In the time of Abraham, Canaan seems to have been undergoing a period of even greater chaos than usual. Its previous network of reasonably prosperous small cities, which could reach fifty acres in size with several thousand citizens, was disintegrating. Some of the cities, along with the settlements near their walls, already lay in abandoned ruin, and the rest were showing signs of decay. The cause of this general collapse of urban centers isn't certain, but prolonged famine rising from multiple years of drought is a reasonable guess. By 2000 BC, more of Canaan's citizens were living in villages or hamlets than in cities, and the number of pastoral nomads was noticeably higher than it had been for a long time.[3] In comparison to Ur and Harran, Canaan was an uncivilized land teetering on the brink of barbarism.

The Land of Canaan derived its name from the dominant tribe of the area: the Canaanites. The tribe claimed descent from Canaan, who was a son of Ham and a grandson of Noah.* Ham, who was one of Noah's three sons, adamantly refused to believe in his father's new Revelation. His refusal (described in chapter 1) was so

---

* Both the Old Testament and the Bahá'í writings describe Canaan as a grandson of Noah.

obstinate that the Qur'án portrays him as being swept away in the great flood:

> As the cauldron of Divine Wrath boiled over, We said to Noah: "Take into the ark a pair, male and female, from each species of domesticated animal, along with all the members of your family save for your wife, whose unbelief is already known to you. Then put all of the believers on the third floor of the ark." But the number of those who believed in Noah's message was small indeed. . . . The ark carried them off, mounting waves as tall as mountains. Seeing his son, who had remained on shore, Noah called out: "My dear son! Embark with us: do not remain among the unbelievers!" Noah's son replied: "I aim to climb a mountain and save myself from the flood!" Noah said: "Today there is nothing that can save men from God's command unless He Himself takes pity on them." At this point a huge wave rose up between Noah and his son, dragging the boy underwater and drowning him along with the rest of the unbelievers.[4]*

When Canaan grew up, he was just as opposed to Noah's Revelation as his spiritually drowned father, Ham, had been. This inherited obstinacy ran so deep, according to the Bahá'í writings, that it had the effect of completely severing Canaan from his noble genetic roots: "It is evident that inherited character also exists, and to such a degree that if the characters are not in conformity with their origin, although they belong physically to that lineage, spiritually they are not considered members of the family; like Canaan, who is not reckoned as being of the race of Noah."[5]

---

* Although many Qur'án commentators suggest that the unnamed "son" who drowned was Canaan, Muḥammad did not give the name of the son. When this is added to the fact that both the Old Testament and Bahá'í scripture agree that Canaan was the grandson—not the son—of Noah, my conclusion is that Ham was the son who was swept away by a tidal wave of disbelief.

Canaan's personal beliefs are not outlined in any scripture, but we do know that his descendants in the Land of Canaan were devoted to the worship of a local god named Baal. He was a god of nature and fertility who ruled agriculture and controlled the weather. Associated with Baal were several other deities, including Mot, the god of death, and Anat, the goddess of war. Each god had its own images before whom the faithful bowed and to whom sacrifices were dedicated.

THE GREAT GOD EL

One's first impression of the religion of Baal is that of unredeemed polytheism, but it's possible to detect a gleam of something infinite hidden amid the muddle of physical idols and limited spirits: the great god El.

A god who was greater than any of the other gods had already been worshipped for a thousand years or more before Abraham was born. The name of the highest god varied from culture to culture, but the concept remained the same—akin to the way that different countries today speak of Gott, Dios, Allah, Jehovah, or Dieu. Those speaking Semitic languages knew him as El, but the Sumerians of lower Mesopotamia had revered him as An, the sky-god of heaven. Akkadians and Assyrians, who also lived in Mesopotamia, referred to him as Anu. Early Egyptians called him Horus, but later dynasties named him Ptah, Atum, or Ra.[6]

In every culture the role of El was the same. He was the father, the progenitor of all the other gods in that particular pantheon. Like the sun in the sky, El ruled in the heavens rather than on the flat earth, and he made the mountains glow at dawn. In the Land of Canaan, El was worshipped under the name of Thoru-El, the "Bull God," and he was revered as the creator of the lesser gods like Baal, Mot, and Anat. Realizing that "the measure of Divine Revelation, in every age, has been adapted to, and commensurate with, the degree of social progress achieved in that age by a constantly evolving humanity," one can conclude that El / Anu / An / Thoru-El was not just any old god. He was the highest god in the universe, no matter the name by which He was called and no matter how poorly He was understood. And, spiritually speaking, this understanding of the highest god was the precursor of the divinity worshipped today as *God, Gott, Dios, Allah, Dieu, Θεός, Deus, Dio, бог, the All-Forgiving, the Lord of Lords.*[7]

With the Revelations of Abraham, Moses, and Jesus, names given to the highest god continued to evolve, and a variety of versions are sprinkled throughout the Old and the New Testaments, though these differences are not usually reflected in standard English translations of the Bible. *Elohim, Elyon, El Ro'i* and *El Shaddai* are four names for God that seem most closely related to the great god El. Enoch, for example "walked with Elohim." Abraham's concubine, Hagar, spoke with El Ro'i, Jacob saw El Shaddai in the land of Canaan, and Melchizedek was a Priest of El Elyon. *El* was also used in combination with another word or two as a way to more clearly express a growing appreciation for all of the different aspects of God, as in *Elohim-Yahweh, Elohim-Yahweh-Adonai,* and *Elohim-Adonai.* The Greeks would eventually adopt El under the name of *Zeus,* and the Romans would accept Him as *Jupiter.* In Arabia, the name would begin as *El-Ilah* and then morph into *Allah.*[8]

It is impossible to say how many different words Jesus used for God, but He is thought to have been fluent in both Hebrew and Aramaic and to have spoken at least a little Greek. He would have learned Hebrew at home in order to read Jewish scripture, but Aramaic was the primary language of Canaan during His life, and Greek was employed by traders and travelers as a common language throughout the Mediterranean world.[9] *Elah* was the most common word for God in Aramaic, while *Theos* and *Kyrios* were Greek equivalents.

Biblical historian Carl Henry allays the fears that people sometimes have about mixing older names for God with newer names by explaining that "in successive periods of redemptive history earlier names of God are retained side by side with later names. Later divine disclosure does not annul the force and significance of the earlier names, for God does not deny himself in the progressive revelation of his names. He can be properly addressed by the earlier or later names."[10]

Abraham's task as a Messenger of God was not to reject or displace El or An or Thoru-El with a new god. It was, rather, to enlarge mankind's spiritual understanding of the infinite Godhead. Polytheism might have been an acceptable way of visualizing spiritual mysteries at previous stages of mankind's existence, but it was time for a change. Abraham's Revelation would enable the world to begin the process of relinquishing its attachment to demigods by introducing the concept of a single God whose immensity could not be (and should not be) represented by a carved or painted image.

Among those who accepted the new understanding about the nature of El / God / Yahweh was Abraham's great-grandson, Joseph. Joseph and his large family became the nucleus of a group of people (usually referred to as *Hebrews*) who moved to Egypt and remained there for more than four centuries—until the advent of Moses. Through their continuing allegiance to the teachings of Abraham, the Hebrews managed to do something very special; they retained their beliefs, their transcendent God, and their separate religious identity—generation after generation—even though they were surrounded by a completely different culture laden with extremely glamorous gods. Their beliefs eventually faltered and had to be rejuvenated by Moses, who sternly reminded them that "You shall have no other gods before Me," and "You shall not make for yourself an idol."[11] Nevertheless, the achievement of the Hebrews in remembering Abraham and retaining at least a slight grip on monotheism in the face of seductive Egyptian polytheism was a memorable achievement.

The Persians, after the Revelation of Zoroaster c. 650 BC, also embraced the concept of one God, but there were still hundreds of places on earth where multiplicity rather than singleness was taken for granted. When the followers of Jesus began taking His Message to the wider world, they often found it necessary to explain, as Paul of Tarsus did, that "handmade gods aren't gods at all."[12] Six hundred years after Jesus, Muḥammad, too, was forced to confront a great number of people—including members of His own tribe—who wanted to close their eyes to the message of intangible oneness and cling, instead, to the comfort of familiar idols.

An Altar with No Gods

In Ur and Haran, Abraham had dramatically demonstrated the foolishness of worshipping idols by smashing them. In the Land of Canaan, He would use a different approach: the unadorned altar.

After entering Canaan, Abraham continued through the land until He arrived at a central spot near Shechem (probably in modern-day Nabulus) where there was a *Moreh*. Variously translated as *hill, plain,* or *tree,* Moreh has the connotation of being associated with a shrine, a sage, a priest, or something of a religious nature. In this case, because Abraham's goal was to spotlight the power of the highest god, the Moreh might have been a hilltop altar dedicated either to Baal or to Thoru-El.

Imagine the scene: Abraham arrives in Shechem and goes to the spot where the chief priests of the area have built an imposing altar (maybe even a ziggurat) and adorned it with idols. Many of the idols are dressed in ceremonial robes, and bowls of food are arranged on the platform in front of them. Priests are chanting praises and accepting sacrificial offerings from onlookers.

As Abraham stands in the middle of this busy throng of people, He sees beyond the bounds of time and place. Because He is a Divine Revelator, He knows with absolute certainty the effect He and His descendants will have on this part of the world. So, as a physical symbol of what the future promises, and as a demonstration of His own faith in God, Abraham ignores the public altar and begins building one of His own nearby.

Because Abraham eschews the use of idols, the new altar appears barren, bizarre, and utterly ridiculous to those who are watching. What, they ask themselves, is the good of an unadorned altar?

To demonstrate the efficacy of the new altar, Abraham uses a ritual that is already familiar in Canaan: He burns a sacrificial offering and offers prayers. Those who see the smoke rise into the air continue to be confused. Without an idol to smell the smoke and accept the sacrifice, how can it have any effect? And, moreover, since Abraham isn't a priest, how can He expect His prayers to be heard?

The Old Testament is quite clear in saying that Abraham built several altars in the Land of Canaan, but, of course, we can't be sure that He used them as a teaching tool in the way described here. Still, it seems quite likely. An unadorned altar would have been a physically meaningful way of communicating Abraham's unshakeable faith in the existence of an all-powerful, all-seeing, and all-hearing, but invisible, God. One or two of those who watched Abraham worshipping in this new style might even have suddenly managed to appreciate the foolishness of having previously put their faith in dead lumps of stone and wood. If so, they might have become the first Canaanite followers of this odd new religion.

By building altars in several different places, which Abraham did as He moved about the land, He conveyed another essential truth: the influence of the one true God was not restricted to a specific spot or a specific altar. He belonged everywhere, could be worshipped from any number of different spots, and could smell the odor of sacrifice wherever it rose.

The notion that a single god could be accessed from many different sites doesn't astonish us now, but it seems to have been a revolutionary idea to Abraham's contemporaries because everyone "knew" that most gods didn't move around much. It was true that a family's household gods might be taken along on a journey to a new home, but they were very minor gods who had only a little bit of influence and were basically owned by the family. All the big powers—the tribal and city gods—were tied to specific cities or certain tribes. A Canaanite would never carry an idol of Baal into new territory and still expect Baal to have any power. If he moved away, he'd have to leave Baal behind in Canaan and adopt the god of the new country. Even El—who did get around a bit more than the others—could only be worshipped in a few special temples through the rituals of acceptable priests.

Bearing these "truths" in mind, it would have been surprising to the Canaanites that Abraham, who had come into Canaan from Ur, continued to venerate the same God that He had known in His previous home. They must also have been shocked to see Him engage in acts of worship without recourse to any of the more familiar priests or idols. And scandalized that Abraham seemed to expect them to abandon Baal and join Him in venerating such a peculiar God.

THE SECOND ALTAR

After Abraham finished His work at the Moreh near Shechem, He moved to a new place and built a second altar at a site described in Genesis as being on the side of a mountain with Bethel to the west and Hai to the east.[13]

There is little agreement about the probable location of this altar, largely due to the ambiguous nature of the descriptive terms: *Bethel* and *Hai*. *Bethel* means *House of El*, or *House of God*, but simply knowing the meaning of the word isn't enough. During Abraham's time in Canaan, there were numerous sites that could have been referred to as a "bethel," and each one would have had its own "house" or temple dedicated to Thoru-El, Baal, or another god. Abraham might have set up an altar near any one of them. *Hai* (also transliterated as *Ai*) is equally obscure because its basic meaning is *heap* or *mass*. Some translators believe that it might have signified a specific ruin that was well-known to the Hebrews but lost to us now, while others believe it might point to a ruin that still exists but hasn't been properly identified.

Another problem that must be faced when thinking about the location of the second altar is the enigmatic nature of the Torah. The first five books of the Old Testament, including Genesis, were not handwritten by Moses, but they do spring directly from His Revelation.* Investigating the verses with appreciative eyes, one is astonished at the magnificent way in which Moses shaped the

---

* The Bahá'í point of view about the origin of the Torah is summed up by 'Abdu'l-Bahá this way: "Know ye that the Torah is that which was revealed in the Tablets to Moses, may peace be upon Him, or that to which He was bidden." ('Abdu'l-Bahá, quoted in a letter written on behalf of the Universal House of Justice, March 13, 1986, in Hornby, *Lights of Guidance*, no. 1683).

events of Abraham's life into a dramatic narrative that transcends the earthly history in which it is rooted.

At its most concrete level, the narrative in the Torah connects the followers of Moses to a noble ancestor named Abraham Who walked where they walked and sacrificed His own comfort for their sakes. At its highest symbolic level, the verses are infused with mystical nuances and prophetic visions that have been a source of wonder, confusion, and delight for millennia. Taking history, mysticism, and prophecy into consideration while simultaneously admitting the lack of physical evidence, one cannot be sure whether the altar between Bethel and Hai, or any Abrahamic altar mentioned by Moses, is tied to a certain latitude and longitude that existed in the past or whether it was intended to weave a connection between Abraham's Revelation and some future event.

The final bit of confusion about Abraham's altars rises from wondering about the rationale behind each of the sites. Did He choose certain locations because of current conditions in His life, or did He seek out sites that would have importance in the future? Did He build them only for the convenience of His own followers or to purposely puzzle the Canaanites? Is it possible that He chose them with full knowledge that several hundred years in the future, Moses would be able to visit the sites, point them out to the Israelites, and thus revive their weakening memories of Abraham? These wonderfully infuriating questions do not, alas, have irrefutable answers.

8

A LESSON FOR PHARAOH

It is He Who revealed the Book to you;
in it there are verses which are of clear, established meaning
and thus fundamental—the cornerstone and foundation
of the book; and there are verses which are allegorical
and thus open to interpretation.
Muḥammad[1]

If, when Abraham built a second altar in Canaan, He again used an absence of idols as a teaching tool, the Torah doesn't mention the immediate effects of His actions. Or perhaps it would be more precise to say that the Book of Genesis has no *explicit* mention of any effects the altar had on those who saw it. What one finds, instead, is an abrupt and somewhat ominous change of scene: "Now there was a famine in the land; so Abram went down to Egypt to sojourn there, for the famine was severe in the land."[2]

The severe famine faced by Abraham in Canaan is often understood as a completely physical event, which geological history indicates is quite possible. Years of plenty followed by years of drought and scarcity were a common routine in that region.

On the other hand, when famine and hunger make an appearance in sacred scripture, they often have mystical implications.[3] A lack of food can indicate spiritual malnourishment rather than bodily starvation. Famine may also be linked to punishment for ingratitude, disobedience, or disbelief. Can it be possible, therefore, that by describing a famine descending on Canaan, scripture is hinting that Abraham's words are falling on deaf ears? That those who hear Him are refusing to accept the nourishing meat of His Revelation? Or, even worse, that Abraham is being persecuted again? Consider the implications of hunger as described in these passages from four different religions:

Judaism: I will send a famine in the land, not a famine of bread, nor a thirst for water, but of hearing the words of the LORD.[4]

Christianity: Jesus said unto them, I am the bread of life: he who comes to me will not hunger; and he who believe in me will never thirst.[5]

Islam: So let them worship the Lord of this House, Who hath fed them against hunger and hath made them safe from fear.[6]

Bahá'í Faith: Verily Thy lovers thirst, O my Lord; lead them to the wellspring of bounty and grace. Verily, they hunger; send down unto them Thy heavenly table. Verily, they are naked; robe them in the garments of learning and knowledge.[7]

To escape the famine, whether of food or faith or both, Abraham and Sarah traveled to the south, through the arid Negev desert, where ancient paths twisted between sharp-edged hills of red stone and mounded dunes of glittering sand. After reaching the Sinai Peninsula, they turned in a more westerly direction and pressed forward into Egypt.

The heart of Egypt, centered on the life-giving Nile River and almost never affected by drought, was green and lush. Soil enriched by the annual flooding of the river produced abundant crops, and Egypt was accustomed to hosting refugees from drier regions.[8]

In addition to plentiful food, Egypt had a long and dazzling history. By the time Abraham arrived, the famous pyramids of Giza had been standing for five centuries, the practice of embalming was more than a thousand years old, and Ra, the sun god, was the primary point of religious worship. Although Egypt had experienced a period of turmoil and divided government in the century prior to Abraham, it had quickly returned to its previous pattern of a strong central government based on a powerful pharaoh surrounded by a bevy of stern priests and advisors. According to the text of Genesis, as Abraham and Sarah approached the city in Egypt where the pharaoh lived, a curious thing happened. Abraham said to Sarah, "Behold now, I know that thou art a fair woman to look upon: Therefore it shall come to pass, when the Egyptians shall see thee, that they shall say, This is his wife: and they will kill me, but they will save thee alive. Say, I pray thee, thou art my sister: that it may be well with me for thy sake; and my soul shall live because of thee."[9]

Sure enough, when they arrived in Egypt, everyone admired Sarah's beauty. Even the palace officials were enchanted, and they sang her praises to the pharaoh. Egypt's ruler, accustomed to having whatever he wanted, decided to appropriate this fascinating woman. By way of compensation, he showered Abraham with a number of gifts, including sheep, cattle, donkeys, servants, and camels.

With any other woman, the story might have ended with a lifetime of confinement. After pleasing the pharaoh for a night or two, she would have been dismissed from his presence and assigned to a chamber in a harem. There, amid dozens (maybe hundreds) of other women she would have lived out the rest of her life, visiting the pharaoh again only if he summoned her, which might be never. She wouldn't starve, and there would be opportunities for communal work, plus entertainment in the form of feasts and celebrations, but she wouldn't have any real freedom, either. High walls kept the royal concubines isolated from the rest of the population, and official overseers were always on hand to make sure the women didn't stray.[10]

Sarah, to the pharaoh's consternation, was not a typical woman. As soon as she was taken into the royal household, the Lord rained plagues down upon the pharaoh. Stricken, the ruler summoned Abraham and questioned Him closely about what had happened. "What have you done to me?" he asked. "Why did you say, 'she is my sister,' so that I took her to be my wife?" Abraham's explanation must have been compelling because, with no further ado, the pharaoh returned Sarah to Abraham. Moreover, he magnanimously insisted that Abraham keep all of the gifts and take them back to Canaan.[11]

Many readers have tried to make sense of this story by rationalizing that God somehow gave Abraham permission to lie about Sarah so that His life would be spared. According to the Bahá'í writings, however, this type of interpretation is not acceptable because it implies that a Messenger of God would be willing to commit a sin. Instead, it would be more plausible to conclude that "Abraham wished to emphasize the superiority of the spiritual relationship binding him with his wife to the purely physical and material one."[12] This spiritual slant on the relationship between Sarah and Abraham is equally affirmed by the way that many biblical translations depict Sarah acting as Abraham's sister so that His *soul* (rather than his physical body) will live. By becoming Abraham's spokesperson in Egypt, Sarah keeps His *soul*—His new Revelation—alive by introducing it into the pharaoh's household.

The notion that a spiritual relationship like the one between Sarah and Abraham could be as important—or even more important—than physical kinship is found in many religions. In Christianity, Jesus describes the bond that exists between people who are mutually devoted to obeying God this way: "For whosoever shall do the will of my Father which is in heaven, the same is my brother, and sister, and mother." Muḥammad echoes this in the Qur'án, saying "The believers are but brothers," or, using a different translation, "The believers are but a single Brotherhood."[13]

In the Muslim hadith (the reported sayings of Muḥammad that are not contained in the Qur'án), the story of Abraham, Sarah, and Pharaoh is straightforwardly linked to the idea of spiritual kinship. Sarah is His *sister* because the two of them are the only true believers in the land:

The Prophet Abraham emigrated with Sarah and entered a village where there was a king or a tyrant. (The king) was told that Abraham had entered (the village) accompanied by a woman who was one of the most charming women. So, the king sent for Abraham and asked, "O Abraham! Who is this lady accompanying you?" Abraham replied, "She is my sister (i.e. in religion)." Then Abraham returned to her and said, "Do not contradict my statement, for I have informed them that you are my sister. By Allah, there are no true believers on this land except you and I." When Pharaoh tried to approach Sarah lustfully, he suffered some sort of fit. Fearing that he would die and that she would be blamed, Sarah prayed that the Pharaoh would be healed. The Pharaoh recovered, tried again to approach Sarah and again was stricken. When he recovered, he promptly returned her to Abraham.[14]

Using the tool of spiritual kinship as a key to unlock the story of Abraham and Sarah's flight to Egypt dramatically changes our understanding of the events. Although it seems on the surface that Abraham was forced to flee from Canaan because of famine, the underlying purpose of the journey must have been that of exposing Egyptians to the new Message from God.

Sarah had already demonstrated her spiritual capacity in Harran, when she had talked about monotheism to other women while Abraham had taught the men. Now, in Egypt, she would have an even more splendid opportunity to spread the new gospel, this time to one of the most powerful men in the world. To assuage any nervousness she might feel about what was going to happen, Abraham reassured her that "my soul shall live because of thee." In other words, the divine power of Abraham's Revelation (His *soul*) would be visible to Pharaoh in the mirror of Sarah's pure and devoted heart.

As Abraham had predicted, Sarah's faith had a powerful effect. Genesis describes it for us in terms of a plague that attacked the pharaoh, but without defining what form it took. Islamic tradition clarifies the matter slightly by adding that when the ruler tried to approach Sarah, he was stricken by either a "mood of agitation," an "epileptic fit," or a "stiff hand."[15]

After adding all the references up, one begins to think that the plagues with which Pharaoh was struck were primarily mental and educatory. Perhaps Sarah's prayers and her explanations of the Revelation of Abraham forced the pharaoh to think about religion in new and very agonizing ways. If so, he might have become so morally agitated by "the plague of his own heart," that he was able to restrain his lust and give Sarah back to Abraham, protesting just a little too loudly that he certainly wouldn't have taken her if he had known she was already married.[16]

Jewish tradition adds credence to the notion that the pharaoh was overwhelmed by the virtuous faith of Sarah and the veracity of the Revelation of Abraham. It notes that after giving Sarah back to Abraham and letting Him keep all of the previous gifts, Pharaoh did something completely unexpected and extra special. He gave one of his daughters—a young woman named Hagar—to serve Sarah as a handmaid. "It is better, my daughter, that you be a servant in the house of Sarah and Abraham, than a princess in some other palace."[17]

Pharaoh must have sired dozens of children by a number of wives and concubines, so it's not as though he gave away his one and only daughter. Still, it's a remarkable act. And, looking ahead several hundred years, it is intriguing to realize that it will be another pharaoh's daughter who will pluck Moses from the bulrushes and raise Him as her own.

9

THE APOSTLE IN SODOM

And, verily, Lot was surely among the apostles . . .
Muḥammad[1]

After their adventures in Egypt, Abraham and Sarah returned to Canaan. With them came the gifts they had been given, including sheep, cattle, and the new handmaid named Hagar. Also with them was Abraham's nephew, Lot, who had grown into manhood under trying circumstances.

Lot was the son of Abraham's youngest brother, Haran. While Lot was young and the whole multigenerational family was still living in Ur, Haran died. When Abraham, Sarah, and Terah were banished from Ur to Harran, Lot accompanied them because, apparently, he had become a believer in the truth of what Abraham had to say. When Abraham was banished from Harran, Lot chose to go into exile with Him in Canaan, where he continued to be faithful to the new Revelation.

As time passed, the flocks of livestock owned by Abraham and Lot grew in size, and so did their households. Both of them, says the Torah, became very rich in "flocks and herds and tents." But, alas, with prosperity came the challenge of finding enough land on which to graze the animals and pitch the tents, and Lot's herdsmen found themselves vying for space with the herdsmen of Abraham. Realizing that "The land could not support them while they stayed together," Abraham made an offer to Lot: In order to avoid strife, one of them should go to a new place. When Lot agreed with the plan, he was given the privilege of deciding whether to be the one who stayed or the one who moved.[2]

DIVIDING THE FLOCKS

In scripture, the word *flock* often refers to something other than a group of animals. It is used to describe a group of believers, as seen in the Book of Psalms when God "made his own people to go forth like sheep, and guided them in the wilderness like a flock."[3] Because this kind of double meaning is likely whenever a flock is mentioned, one suspects that the Torah is providing hints about the growth of Abraham's new religion. Evidently Abraham and Lot had succeeded in making a number of converts to monotheism—so many converts that they could not possibly all live together as a single unit—and it became necessary for a "flock" of them to move to new territory.

The way in which Abraham and Lot are forced into moving apart can be viewed as both a physical necessity and a spiritual imperative. Physically, some of the animals need new fields on which to graze, or they will starve. Spiritually, the religion is ready to spread out into fresh pastures and convert new souls, if those souls are willing.

LOT CHOOSES A FIELD

Abraham's apostle, Lot, offers to be the one who will move away and take a flock into fresh territory. He has the spiritual dedication that will enable him to cling to his beliefs in a new situation where skepticism will be the norm. He is married and either already has—or will soon have—children, which gives him the hope of being the founder of a tribe that will also follow Abraham and continue to pass His religion on to new generations.

When Lot is trying to decide where to go on his mission trip, he realizes that the region around the Jordan River is "well-watered, like the garden of the Lord, like the land of Egypt."[4] This beautiful vision of abundant water in an arid land makes it tempting to think about the verse in literal terms, but physical water is not the only thing that Lot sees. If he is gazing out across the land with eyes of faith, with eyes that see the cycles of religion, he is looking not just at the Jordan but at the Middle East in general, an arena in which spiritually important things have happened and will continue to happen.

The land that Lot sees has already been "well-watered" through the actions of Abraham's predecessors, including Adam and Noah, who sprinkled the Middle East with the Word of God. In the future—even after Abraham and Lot have both died—the region will continue to be showered with drops of divine Revelation: Moses will be born in Egypt and emigrate to ancient Israel. Zoroaster will live in Iran. Jesus will be born in ancient Israel, will visit Egypt, and will be baptized with water from the Jordan River. Muḥammad will live His whole life in Arabia. The Báb will be born in Iran, but after His martyrdom, His remains will be entombed in Canaan / Israel. Bahá'u'lláh will be born in Iran, travel through Iraq, Syria, and Turkey, and live more than a third of His life in what is now Israel.

Unfortunately, *well-watered* does not equal *well-received.* The lands honored by receiving divine Revelations have always raised strenuous objections to the new guidance. The *Garden of the Lord* (i.e., the Garden of Eden) was certainly a blessed spot, yet it was also the place where man turned away from God's guidance and ate the fruit of "the tree of the knowledge of good and evil." Ancient Israel was well-watered, but it opposed Jesus and facilitated His crucifixion. Arabia was well-watered but persecuted Muḥammad. Persia was well-watered but resisted Zoroaster, martyred the Báb, and expelled Bahá'u'lláh. Moses was born in Egypt, but it opposed the new Word of God so adamantly that He and His followers were forced to flee.[5]

Lot, a brave apostle, remains undaunted by the dangers inherent in taking the news of Abraham's Revelation to a place reminiscent of Eden and Egypt. He moves to the lush region of promise / peril and pitches his tent, an act that is more than just a comment on housekeeping. In a spiritual sense, facing a tent in a certain direction is an invitation to a specific group of people to investigate one's religion. Lot boldly orients his tent toward Sodom, a city filled with men who "were wicked and sinners before the Lord exceedingly."[6]

WAR

Soon after Lot pitches his tent toward Sodom, he becomes a prisoner of war. The fracas begins when Sodom, Gomorrah, and two other nearby settlements are attacked by a group of four Syrian kings. Sodom and Gomorrah fall, and both of them are looted. Many of the local inhabitants are taken as prisoners—probably destined to serve as slaves when the armies get back to Syria—and Lot is among the captives. When an escapee manages to find Abraham and tell Him what has happened, Abraham recruits a band of fighters from among the men of His household. They pursue the raiders, attack them by night, and recover Lot as well as the other captives and the stolen valuables.

As soon as Abraham returns with Lot and the loot, He is met by a group of grateful local rulers. One of them is the king of Sodom, who thanks Abraham by offering to let Him keep all of the goods He has recovered. Abraham lets His fighters take a share of the wealth as repayment for their efforts, but He Himself refuses to accept anything, explaining the refusal with a quiet hint about the ignoble nature of Sodom's king: "I have solemnly promised the Lord God Most High, Creator of heaven and earth, that I will not take so much as a single thread or sandal thong from you. Otherwise, you might say 'I am the one who made [Abraham] rich.'"[7]

What Abraham does accept, by contrast, is a blessing from a mysterious king who suddenly materializes among the other rulers who have come to celebrate the victory. The king, named Melchizedek, approaches Abraham, gives him bread and wine, and blesses Him in the name of the "God Most High, Creator of heaven and earth."[8]

MELCHIZEDEK, KING OF SALEM

The Torah and the New Testament agree that Melchizedek is not an ordinary king. He is, rather, a "priest of the most high God" who is "Without father, without mother, without genealogy, having neither beginning of days nor end of life . . ."[9] Even his name is symbolic because *Melchizedek* means *king of righteousness* and the place where he rules—*Salem*—is the *place of peace.*

When Melchizedek blesses Abraham and feeds him wine and bread, it can be understood as a transcendent symbol of the way in which the Holy Spirit has been conferred upon Abraham in His role as a Messenger of God. In a subsequent age, the same thing will happen to Jesus; He will be anointed by the Holy Spirit / King of Righteousness / Melchizedek, and will join Abraham in becoming "another priest" who has spiritual authority "according to the order of Melchizedek."[10]

The bread and wine used by Melchizedek are destined to become symbols of enlightenment and remembrance in two major religions: Judaism and Christianity. After candles are lit to brighten the Sabbath evening, Jews will celebrate their covenant with God by drinking from a cup of red wine or grape juice and eating a braided loaf of challah bread. Christians will partake of bread and wine during the ritual of communion, using the mouthful of physical nourishment as an embodiment of the spiritual sustenance provided by Jesus.

After being blessed, Abraham tithes a tenth of the spoils of war to Melchizedek, an act of respect that demonstrates by example the way in which one might want to give a portion of one's possessions to one's religion. Abraham does not—as far as we know—turn this act into a law for His followers, but it is one of the scriptural incidents on which the subsequent practice of tithing will be based.[11]

After the war is over and peace reigns, Lot and his family return to Sodom. His wife is happy with the city, enjoying the comforts and amusements it offers. Their children—two daughters—grow old enough to marry and become engaged to local men. Although Lot doesn't make any progress in converting local residents to the religion of Abraham, he is not necessarily unhappy with the prospect of spending the rest of his life there.

10

PROMISES, PROMISES

Verily, God will not depart from His promise.
Muḥammad[1]

While Lot is engaged with his mission of ministering to the "wicked and sinners" in Sodom, Abraham continues to receive promises about the future of His family line. Though still childless, He is given to understand that His seed will be "as the dust of the earth; so that if a man can number the dust of the earth, then shall thy seed also be numbered." Specifically, Abraham is promised a son who will "come forth out of thine own bowels" or, as some translations have it, "who will come forth from your own body." It is important to note here that it could be any son about whom the promise is made—not necessarily the child of His current wife, Sarah.[2]

Abraham also hears that the land will be part of the inheritance of His descendants. He is portrayed as not being convinced by the promise about the land because He asks, "O Lord God, how am I to know that I shall possess it?" The Lord replies, "Bring me a heifer, a goat and a ram, each three years old, along with a dove and a young pigeon."[3]

Abraham gathers the animals as directed and cuts them in two. He lays the halves of the big animals on top of each other, but He doesn't cut the birds in two. Gory, isn't it? Blood and guts everywhere. But the true point of this portion of the story might be one of several things: First, this kind of effort indicates a willingness to sacrifice oneself in the path of God. Abraham has already thrown Himself into the fires of polytheism in order to respond to the call of God, and has taken His Revelation to a new land—Canaan— that is spiritually deficient. As the Bahá'í writings point out, "In reality, Abraham sacrificed Himself, for He brought heavenly teachings to the world and conferred heavenly food upon mankind."[4]

Another way to appreciate the significance of the dead animals is to realize that Abraham isn't performing a traditional sacrifice because there isn't an altar. Instead, He is *cutting a covenant*—a Hebrew idiom based on cultural practices of the time. To cut a covenant, the two people who were making an agreement would take one or two large animals and cut them in half. After this was done, each of the two parties to the covenant would walk between the halves. The purpose of this was to publicly obligate both people to suffering the same fate—being cut in half—if they violated the agreement.[5]

A third thing that might be fluttering around the bestial images is prophecy. The large animals have been taken by some commentators as representing the different kingdoms that would overpower the land and the people of Israel, including Babylon, Persia, and Greece. Because the birds on top of the pile remain uncut, it could mean that the violence won't come to an end until, the Talmud suggests, the Jews return to their homeland, the Messiah comes, and a third temple is built by the dynasty of David.* In that view, the story is connected to our own time because Jews have returned to their homeland of Palestine / Israel.[6]

A fourth possibility—also in the realm of prophecy—is that the five animals and birds represent the five religions that will come

---

* The first temple was built in Jerusalem by King Solomon circa 1000 BC. It was destroyed by Babylonian invaders, rebuilt circa 538 BC, and then destroyed again in AD 70 by Roman soldiers. The third temple would replace these two destroyed temples.

from the line of Abraham: Judaism, Christianity, Islam, the Bábí Faith, and the Bahá'í Faith. The hacked and bleeding animals on the bottom represent the animosities that will arise among the religions and the blood that will be shed by their followers. But the two uncut birds on the top signify an end to the cycle of interfaith violence and the coming together of all of the lines of descendants in peace.

Returning to the bloody scene, we see something else happen: As the butchered animals lie there, ready for someone to walk between them and ratify the covenant, winged predators swoop down upon the carcasses. Symbolism again, by any chance? Do these birds of prey signify spiritual enemies, ready to swoop down and disturb the functioning of this new covenant? Can the ferocious birds be compared to the pharaoh who pursued Moses, the crucifiers of Jesus, the enemies of Muḥammad, and the persecutors of the Báb and Bahá'u'lláh?

Abraham drives the birds away, indicating that the Covenant is safe. Shortly after that, night descends. Abraham falls asleep and has a nightmarish vision of the future:

> As the sun was setting, Abram fell into a deep sleep, and a thick and dreadful darkness came over him. Then the Lord said to him: "Know for certain that your descendants will be strangers in a country not their own, and they will be enslaved and mistreated four hundred years. But I will punish the nation they serve as slaves, and afterward they will come out with great possessions. You, however, will go to your fathers in peace and be buried at a good old age. In the fourth generation your descendants will come back here [Canaan] for the sin of the Amorites has not yet reached its full measure."[7]

The dream of Abraham became reality when some of His descendants moved to Egypt, fell on hard times, were forced to serve its government until finally extricated by Moses, and then, under the leadership of Joshua, returned to Canaan and managed to become the rulers of its people. Historians take the reference to the Amorites to mean the indigenous population of Canaan because the writers of the Bible often used *Amorites* interchangeably with *Canaanites*.[8] The "sin" of these people in reference to Abraham would indicate their continuing resistance to Abraham and to monotheism in the years between the death of Abraham and the flowering of the Revelation of Moses.

The story of the bloody covenant ends with a formal ratification of the agreement: "When the sun had set and darkness had fallen, a smoking firepot with a blazing torch appeared and passed between the pieces."[9]

Intriguingly, the ratification process doesn't involve any human beings at all. Not a single person walks between the bloody halves of the animals. Instead, two objects—variously translated as a *smoking furnace or firepot* or *oven* plus a *burning lamp,* a *blazing torch,* or a *torch of fire*—pass between the pieces. A torch is easy to visualize, but a firepot is more difficult because modern society has replaced it with matches, butane lighters, and spark plugs. A firepot was a clay or metal pot, usually small enough to be portable, that had some ventilation as well as a lid. In it, a very slow-burning fire or bed of coals could be kept going (kept *smoking*) almost indefinitely by the regular addition of small amounts of wood or other fuel. Firepots were a clever means of being prepared to ignite a cooking fire, a campsite blaze, or even a torch whenever needed.

The way in which a smoking firepot and blazing torch are used to ratify this very special covenant may well symbolize the manner in which God will continue to reveal Himself through Abraham's descendants. Time and time again, the Holy Spirit, like a trusty firepot, will ignite the blazing torch of a new religion to illumine the dark night of spiritual ignorance and error.

As the covenant is ratified, God speaks again, saying, "To your descendants I have given this land, From the river of Egypt as far as the great river, the river Euphrates."[10]

In considering, not for the first time, who the inheriting descendants of Abraham will be, one finds that there is still no mention of a specific child by a specific wife. Astonishingly, Abraham has no children at all when the covenant is made. The only clear promise is that the land in question will stretch from the Nile River to the east until it hits the Euphrates River, which runs from the eastern part of Turkey down into Iraq. This description of the land varies a bit from other descriptions found in the Old Testament and will be examined further in chapter 24. Right now, though, we will move ahead and take a peek at the life of the woman who is slated to become the mother of Abraham's first, ardently cherished, son.

11

ASTONISHED BY AN ANGEL

It takes two to speak the truth, —
one to speak and another to hear.
Henry David Thoreau[1]

The next part of Genesis—Chapter 16—opens with the news that "Sarai, Abram's wife, had borne him no children."[2] Because Sarah has been barren since the beginning of her marriage, and because—as scripture suggests—Abraham needs children to continue the line of inheritance, she approaches Him with a suggestion.

"Behold," Sarah says, "Behold now, the LORD hath restrained me from bearing: I pray thee, go in unto my maid; it may be that I may obtain children by her."[3] Sarah makes this generous offer because it was the custom—perhaps even the law—that a wife who couldn't produce children was obligated to find a second wife with whom the husband could try to beget children. When the baby was born, it would become the adopted child of the first wife and, if male, would become her husband's heir. And that is how Hagar, the Egyptian, who was perhaps a daughter of a pharaoh, found herself in the position of assuming wifely duties in regard to Abraham.

No one has recorded Hagar's reaction to being pushed into the position of becoming a mother, but Abraham agrees to the arrangement. Conception takes place on—tradition says—the very first night, and over the next several months, Genesis outlines a drama worthy of the most imaginative soap opera. As soon as Hagar is sure she's pregnant, she becomes contemptuous of Sarah and behaves badly toward her.

What did Hagar do? Scripture is mute, but Jewish sources give this account: Hagar is having a difficult time with her pregnancy, and Sarah is concerned. So, when friends stop by to visit Sarah, she asks them to visit Hagar, too. Hagar, rather than being grateful to Sarah for the extra attention, begins denigrating her. She is even bold enough to suggest that Sarah's barren condition is due to her lack of spirituality. "My lady Sarah is not inwardly what she appears to be outwardly. She makes the impression of a righteous, pious woman, but she is not, for if she were, how could her childlessness be explained after so many years of marriage, while I became pregnant at once?"[4]

Whether due to backbiting or something else, the unpleasantness between Sarah and Hagar becomes so annoying that Sarah complains to Abraham. He refuses to take sides, replying that because Sarah is the mistress of the household, she has the right to do what she pleases with her servant.

The upshot, Genesis reports, is that Sarah deals harshly with Hagar. What kind of thing does this mean? What did she do? Historical evidence indicates that if a wife gave a servant to her husband as a concubine, and if this servant subsequently claimed equality with her mistress because she bore children, the mistress could exact retribution by demoting the woman to her former station as servant. Plus, if the concubine spoke insolently to her mistress, her mouth could be scrubbed out with a quart of salt.

Tradition paints an even more vivid picture: Sarah removes a slipper, slaps Hagar with it, and then forbids Hagar to sleep with Abraham any longer.

In considering the animosity between the wives, should we presume that none of this happened literally? Is the antagonism sketched out in Genesis between wife and concubine not really about the women of four thousand years ago but primarily a sad prophecy of the attitudes that many of the descendants of Abraham will have toward one another?

Whatever the mystical truth of the matter, the result of the disagreement as witnessed in the Old Testament is that Hagar runs away. She turns to the south and begins following a path across the wilderness—the Negev desert and the Sinai Peninsula—separating her from her native land of Egypt.* Considered physically, Hagar is doing what many young women do in difficult circumstances; she's running home to mama. Considered mystically, Hagar is abandoning monotheism and returning to the polytheistic faith she knew as a child. Or, using the symbolism about Egypt that was contained in Lot's story, Hagar is headed to a place that has been *well-watered* but has resisted accepting a new Revelation from God.

While Hagar is in the wilderness, she sits down to rest near a gushing spring of water. While she is resting, she is approached by a visitor and given a message that will change her life: "And the angel of the LORD found her by a fountain of water in the wilderness . . . And he said, Hagar, Sarai's maid, whence camest thou? and whither wilt thou go? And she said, I flee from the face of my mistress Sarai. And the angel of the LORD said unto her, Return to thy mistress, and submit thyself under her hands."[5]

This astonishing event firmly establishes Hagar's importance. It is the very first appearance of an angel in the Bible and one of only four occurrences of an angel speaking with a woman. After visiting Hagar, hundreds of years will pass before a second visit to a woman, when the honor will go to the mother of Samson. The third appearance will be to Mary, the mother of Jesus. The fourth biblical appearance is not to a single woman but to a group of them, including Mary Magdalene, who enter the cave where Jesus' body is entombed. That's it.

In visualizing Hagar's angel, it would be viscerally satisfying to sketch an outline of the unearthly creature on a piece of paper,

---

* Genesis Shur, the place mentioned in connection with the path of Hagar's flight, is thought to be in a desert area of the Sinai peninsula.

but a thorough reading of scripture frustrates any such attempt. The characteristics assigned to these extraterrestrial beings are too contradictory to be captured by pen, pencil, or brush. Angels are creatures fashioned of fire, yet they are also flying seraphim with six wings as well as awesome apparitions with faces like lightning. They occasionally have the features of a man, are sometimes dressed in dazzling robes, and at least one model comes complete with feet that gleam like burnished bronze. No two, it would seem, are alike.*

Furthermore, an angel is not created from earthly clay. It is, as both the Old and New Testaments subtly but surely point out, an ethereal "vision" that one cannot see or appreciate without experiencing a spiritual awakening that has "opened the eyes." In the Bahá'í writings, angels are described as "the confirmations of God and His celestial powers." The word is also used to refer to people who have become so spiritual that they have "severed all ties with this nether world, have been released from the chains of self and the desires of the flesh, and anchored their hearts to the heavenly realms of the Lord." These words suggest that angelic images are used in sacred scripture as a means of imparting heavenly truths, revealing glimpses of the future, or vivifying otherwise inexplicable mystical experiences. One should not, therefore, expect to capture the fluttering of an angel's wing on even the most sophisticated of cameras.[6]

When Hagar is visited by an angel, she is encountering spiritual truth in a form too powerful for her to deny. She understands her responsibility and realizes that Egypt is not her destiny. She will have to return to the tent of Abraham and Sarah: "And the angel of the LORD said unto her, Return to thy mistress, and submit thyself under her hands."[7]

Enthralled by the angelic voice, Hagar realizes she will have a boy whose name will reflect the fact that God has heard and understood her troubles: "And the angel of the LORD said to her, Be-

---

* Varying descriptions of angels can be found in Exodus 3:2 (New Living Translation), Isaiah 6:2 (New Living Translation), Daniel 10:5–6 (New Revised Standard Version), Qur'án 35:1 (Yusuf Ali), and Luke 24:4 (New Living Translation).

hold, you are with child and shall bear a son, and shall call his name Ishmael; because the LORD has heard your affliction."[8] Ishmael, in translation, means *God hears*.

Hagar is given to understand that through Ishmael, she will have many descendants. The "angel of the LORD said unto her, I will multiply thy seed exceedingly, that it shall not be numbered for multitude."[9] This echoes the promise already received by Abraham, that His descendants will be multitudinous.

Hagar also learns from the angel what the life of her son will be like. The description of Ishmael isn't one that most mothers would find comforting, though looking at four translations gives a better sense of the message being conveyed.

> He will be a wild donkey of a man, His hand will be against everyone, And everyone's hand will be against him; And he will live to the east of all his brothers.[10]

> And he will be a wild man; his hand will be against every man, and every man's hand against him; and he shall dwell in the presence of all his brothers.[11]

> He will be a wild donkey of a man; his hand will be against everyone and everyone's hand against him, and he will live in hostility toward all his brothers.[12]

> And he will be a wild ass of a man—his hand against all, the hand of all against him, he will encamp in despite of all his kin.[13]

Taking the information apart phrase by phrase, it is intriguing to learn that the *wild ass* or *wild donkey* reference may be an idiom that is not connected with innate character but indicates that Ishmael and his descendants will, like a wandering wild donkey, lead a nomadic rather than a settled life.[14]

In the phrase describing Ishmael's hand as being "against every man and every man's hand against him," the Hebrew word used for *hand* has an underlying sense of power and movement in a certain direction. Thus the phrase could indicate the problems that Ishmael (and his descendant, Muḥammad) will encounter when preaching monotheism to tribes who resist the movement toward one God. He will push the powerful hand of belief toward them, but they will push back against him.

As for living "to the east" or "in the presence of" or "in hostility toward" his brothers, the differing versions demonstrate just how strongly one's bias can influence a translation and how perilous it can be to rely on a single point of view. The original Hebrew idiom is *'al pěnê*, an expression that literally means *before the face of* or *in front of* and does not necessarily carry an overtone of hostility or conflict.[15] *'Al pěnê* can also have a geographic connotation, and that is the understanding used by translators who indicate that Ishmael will live "to the east" of Canaan, which is where Arabia is. Others simply indicate that he will be "in the presence of" his brothers. A few, like the relatively recent New International Version, seem much more eager to interpret the original idiom in light of current world problems, and they have decided that Ishmael's descendants will live "in hostility" with the religions founded by his brothers. Others take exactly the opposite approach, feeling Ishmael is destined to live and survive in spite of encroachments made by his brethren—i.e., he will "encamp in despite of his kin."

Hagar is astonished by her encounter with divine truth in the form of an angel, and she calls out to the heavens in wonder, shocked that God has seen her. She is so surprised to have survived such a disquieting event that she asks, "Have I even stayed alive after seeing him?"[16]

In gratitude and in recognition of the truth of the existence of God, Hagar gives the spring of water by which she has rested a name: Beerlahairoi, "The well of the Living One, my beholder."[17] And then she heeds the advice she has received. Hagar returns to her mistress, Sarah, and bears a son, whom she names Ishmael.

12

THE SECOND HEIR

*Is there, of the sounds that float
Unsighingly, a single note
Half so sweet and clear and wild
As the laughter of a child?*
Laman Blanchard[1]

After the birth of Ishmael, several exciting things happen.

First, God reaffirms the existing covenant with Abraham, reminding Him that His descendants will be made into a mighty nation. This matches and reaffirms the promise Hagar has received for Ishmael. Abraham, overwhelmed and grateful at the blessings in store for His son, prostrates himself in the dust. But, just as things seem settled, there is a surprise. God reveals that the nation to be born through Abraham's heir, Ishmael, will not be the only nation founded by Abraham's descendants.

What is more, Ishmael will no longer be Abraham's only son. Ishmael will soon have a half-brother because it is now Sarah's turn to have a baby. Like Hagar, Sarah will receive blessings through her descendants because "she shall be a mother of nations; kings of peoples shall be of her."[2]

As a sign of His promise, God provides a new name for the Messenger of God. His birth name of *Abram* becomes *Abraham*. At first glance, there seems hardly any difference between *Abram* and *Abraham*. But although both names have the connotation of *exalted father*, the slight change enlarges the meaning to reflect the terms of this new covenant. *Abraham* means *father of a multitude.*[3]

Abraham's wife also receives a new name. Sarai is renamed *Sarah*. In the view of many linguists, *Sarai* means *noble* or *royal* or even *princess* in the sense that a father might call his daughter *my little princess*. An alternate explanation is that *Sarai* is based on a root word that means *quarrelsome* or *contentious,* which is exactly how it is explained on many Web sites dedicated to the process of naming a baby.

Sarai's new name, *Sarah*, is almost always explained as having the connotation of *Princess* with a capital *P,* though a few people hold out for the idea that it is taken from an Arabic root—*saraa*—and means *having numerous progeny*. In either case, the bestowal of a new name can be seen as a recognition of Sarah's spiritual capacity as well as an indication of the lasting effect she will have on humanity. Four thousand years later, Sarah continues to be a very popular name, and she is still referred to as a woman who "glorified the human race" by her excellences.[4]

In return for all these blessings, God announces that succeeding generations must be faithful to Him. He also prophesies that the land of Canaan will eventually be given to Abraham and His offspring. Because some translations of the verses in Genesis describing the covenant are puzzling, it can be useful to read at least two translations and compare them. Here is one in modern American English:

> "I will make a covenant with you, by which I will guarantee to make you into a mighty nation." At this, Abram fell face down in the dust. Then God said to him, "This is my covenant with you. I will make you the father of not just one nation, but a multitude of nations! What's more, I am changing your name. It will no longer be Abram; now you will be known as Abraham, for you will be the father of many nations. I will give you millions of descendants who will represent many nations. Kings will be among them!

"I will continue the everlasting covenant between us, generation after generation. It will continue between me and your offspring forever. And I will always be your God and the God of your descendants after you. Yes, I will give all this land of Canaan to you and to your offspring forever."[5]

Here is another translation, in more formal British English:

And I will make my covenant between me and thee, and will multiply thee exceedingly. And Abram fell on his face: and God talked with him, saying, As for me, behold, my covenant is with thee, and thou shalt be a father of many nations. Neither shall thy name any more be called Abram, but thy name shall be Abraham; for a father of many nations have I made thee. And I will make thee exceeding fruitful, and I will make nations of thee, and kings shall come out of thee.

And I will establish my covenant between me and thee and thy seed after thee in their generations for an everlasting covenant, to be a God unto thee, and to thy seed after thee. And I will give unto thee, and to thy seed after thee, the land wherein thou art a stranger, all the land of Canaan, for an everlasting possession; and I will be their God.[6]

Abraham is described as laughing at the idea that he and Sarah can have a child this late in life. To emphasize their ages, Abraham is said to be ninety-nine and Sarah ten years younger. But, as usual, we don't really know how old the two of them were in solar years, though a good guess would be middle-aged. Not too old for children by today's standards, but quite old in a society where women were generally expected to bear at least one child before the age of twenty. God, amusingly, acknowledges the humor of the situation by directing Abraham to call the son *Isaac*, which means *he laughs*.

One would suppose that the announcement of the advent of Isaac and the wonderful covenant that has come into being between God and the descendants of Isaac would call for a celebration. Instead, Abraham becomes concerned that His first son, Ishmael, the cherished child born of Hagar, will now be ignored in favor of Isaac. Perhaps, Abraham worries, Ishmael will die early or be left out of the blessings after Isaac is born. As a loving father, Abraham pleads with God about the fate of Ishmael, saying, "O that Ishmael might live before thee!" or, in another translation, "If only Ishmael might live under your blessing."[7]

To allay Abraham's fears, God reaffirms the blessings that will be bestowed upon Ishmael and outlines them in even greater detail. "And as for Ishmael," God says, "I have heard thee (remember the pun in this phrase; Ishmael means "God hears"); Behold, I have blessed him, and will make him fruitful, and will multiply him exceedingly; twelve princes shall he beget, and I will make him a great nation." Having reassured Abraham that all the promises made to Ishmael will be fulfilled, God continues, "But my covenant I will establish with Isaac, whom Sarah will bear to you at this season next year." The agreement with Isaac is not intended to be a short one because, God explains, ". . . I will establish my covenant with him for an everlasting covenant, and with his seed after him.[8]

The elaborate and everlasting covenant with Isaac is sealed with a sacrifice, just as the first covenant was. This time, though, the sacrifice is quite different. No animals or birds are needed. Instead, God says, "Every male among you shall be circumcised. You shall be circumcised in the flesh of your foreskins and it shall be a sign of the covenant between me and you." All the males in Abraham's camp are to be circumcised, and newborns will undergo the procedure when they are eight days old. Abraham obediently seals the covenant as directed: "And Abraham took Ishmael his son, and all that were born in his house, and all that were bought with his money, every male among the men of Abraham's house; and circumcised the flesh of their foreskin in the selfsame day, as God had said unto him. And Abraham was ninety years old and nine, when he was circumcised in the flesh of his foreskin. And Ishmael his son was thirteen years old, when he was circumcised in the flesh of his foreskin."[9]

The Value of Circumcision

Before the time of Abraham, there were already places in the world, including Australia and Egypt, where young men were routinely circumcised, probably as a symbol of passage into adulthood.[10] The law given by Abraham differed from these customs because it was applied to babies. The initial circumcision, of course, was of the older males in Abraham's household, but when Isaac was born, he was circumcised on the eighth day of his life, thus setting a pattern for when the operation should be performed. The law included the provision that in the generations to come, any male whose foreskin was not circumcised would be cut off from his people for breaking the covenant, a mandate that had the effect of ensuring that devout parents would circumcise their babies.

From that time on, circumcision of male babies as a sign of the continuing covenant between God and man began to be practiced among the followers of Abraham, and it continued among the followers of Moses. It is thought that at least some of the Arabs who descended from Ishmael also practiced circumcision, though it is not clear if Muḥammad was circumcised or not.[11] After Muḥammad's death, many of His followers took up the practice of circumcision as a sign of their understanding of the relationship between Abraham and Muḥammad—even though Muḥammad Himself did not comment on circumcision in the Qur'án. Currently, circumcision is the norm in most Muslim countries.

In pondering the rationale behind the rite of male circumcision (female circumcision, by contrast, is never mentioned or condoned in any of the divine scriptures), one wonders why such a traumatic procedure was chosen, especially since the child on whom it is performed has no say in the matter. If the child can't agree or disagree, the involuntary act cannot be taken as a sign of his own belief. A few hundred years after Abraham, in fact, the prophet Jeremiah made it clear that true circumcision has nothing to do with flesh and everything to do with the state of one's soul by saying, "Circumcise yourselves to the LORD, and take away the foreskins of your heart . . ." The New Testament makes an even more dramatic declaration by swearing that men who have never been circumcised can be counted as believers if their faith is real: "In him you were also circumcised, in the putting off of the sinful nature, not with a circumcision done by the hands of men but with the circumcision done by Christ . . ."[12]

It is possible that Abraham chose circumcision simply because His followers would need, over the next few centuries, a dramatic rite by which to remember their relationship to the covenant and to the Revelation of Abraham. Circumcision certainly serves as a powerful tool for connecting the heart of a father—who sympathizes completely with the cries of his baby—to the heart of Abraham when He heard the cries of His own children.

But, aside from all the drama and symbolism, valuable though they might be in establishing a group's religious identity, there is another excellent reason why Abraham might have chosen circumcision rather than a tattoo or some other mark of faith. Circumcising males when they are just a few days old turns out to be an extremely effective public health measure. Large medical studies done in the late twentieth century revealed a purely physical side-benefit that the American Urological Association sums up this way: "For the first three to six months of life, the incidence of urinary tract infections is at least ten times higher in uncircumcised than circumcised boys."[13]

In a pre-antibiotic age, urinary-tract infections could easily kill a baby or damage the kidneys of those who survived. The followers of Abraham who faithfully circumcised their boys would have been rewarded with healthier babies and a higher survival rate than groups who didn't practice early circumcision, even though they wouldn't have been aware of the science behind the survival.

A second physical benefit is that men who are circumcised as infants have a lower rate of penile cancer later in life. A third advantage—discovered only recently—is that in areas where condoms are not routinely used, circumcised males are less likely to contract sexually transmitted diseases because "circumcision reduces the rate of infection by 50 to 60%."[14]

THREE VISITORS

After the covenant with Isaac has been fully described and sealed with circumcision—but before the actual birth of Isaac—Abraham receives three unexpected visitors who arrive during the heat of the day. Or, looking more carefully at the story, the Lord, accompanied by two men, comes to visit Abraham: "And the LORD appeared unto him in the plains of Mamre: and he sat in the tent door in the heat of the day; And he lift up his eyes and looked, and, lo, three men stood by him: and when he saw them, he ran to meet them from the tent door, and bowed himself toward the ground," saying, "if I have found favor in your eyes, my lord, do not pass your servant by."[15]

Sarah and Abraham welcome the visitors and prepare a feast for them. After the feast, one of the visitors begins chatting with Sarah. He informs her that he will visit again in a year, at which time she will have a son. The information about the impending conception of Isaac isn't new information because the covenant between God and Isaac has already been made known to Sarah and Abraham. Why, then, is the birth of Isaac mentioned, and what is the purpose of these men? As straightforward visitors, they don't make sense. In many ways, they don't even seem to be fully human. Interpretations abound, from the theory that these men have been sent to test Abraham's goodness (he passes the test by preparing food for them) to the notion that "these angel visitors symbolize the trinity."[16]

Another prophetic interpretation emerges from the viewpoint expressed by St. Augustine, who notes that although Abraham saw three men, he addressed them as though they were one, bowing before them and saying "Lord (singular), do not pass your servant by." According to Augustine, there was something about the three men that one "could not doubt that God was in them as he was wont to be in the prophets."[17] If God was *in* all three men, then it is possible to infer that they are not men but Messengers of God, and that their visit is a portent of things to come. In that case, the angelic visitors represent the three Messengers who will be descendants of Isaac—Moses, Jesus, and Bahá'u'lláh.

13

ANGELS IN SODOM

Sleep, my love, and peace attend thee
All through the night;
Guardian angels, God will lend thee,
All through the night.
Welsh folksong[1]

After the three mysterious visitors have finished talking with Sarah and Abraham about Sarah's impending pregnancy, they set off to visit Lot, who is still doing his best to preach the new gospel to the wicked inhabitants of Sodom. Abraham decides to accompany them part of the way.

As the men walk, they begin to discuss the fate of Sodom, and the Lord says to Abraham, "The outcry against Sodom and Gomorrah is so great and their sin so grievous that I will go down and see if what they have done is as bad as the outcry that has reached me." He indicates that if the condition of the cities is as bad as it seems, destruction will ensue. Abraham is so disconcerted by this idea that He stops walking. The Lord stays with Him, but the other two men—who from now on will be described as *angels* in the Torah—keep walking.

To find out whether it is truly necessary to destroy Sodom and Gomorrah, Abraham begins posing questions. "Will you destroy both innocent and guilty alike?" He asks. "Suppose you find fifty innocent people there within the city—will you still destroy it, and not spare it for their sakes? Surely you wouldn't do such a thing, destroying the innocent and the guilty exactly the same! Surely you wouldn't do that! Should not the Judge of all the earth do what is right?"

The Lord responds to Abraham by saying, "If I find fifty innocent people in Sodom, I will spare the entire city for their sake."

Abraham chides Himself for being arrogant enough to argue with the Lord but then immediately escalates the argument: "Now that I have been so bold as to speak to the Lord, though I am nothing but dust and ashes," He says, "what if the number of the righteous is five less than fifty? Will you destroy the whole city because of five people?"

"If I find forty-five there," the Lord replies, "I will not destroy it."

Abraham is not content with forty-five. He asks what will happen if there are thirty innocents . . . and then twenty . . . and, finally, "What if only ten can be found there?"

"For the sake of ten I will not destroy it," the Lord responds. With this, the conversation ends, and Abraham returns to his home.[2]

THE POWER OF INNOCENCE

By means of His argument with the Lord, Abraham introduces a new spiritual concept to mankind: the protective power that can be generated by the choices of a single individual or by a very small group of individuals.

The existence of moral choice had certainly been demonstrated by Adam and Eve and their interaction with the fruit tree of the knowledge of good and evil, and by the flood associated with Noah; yet as far as can be gleaned from scripture, the positive spiritual power generated by a single individual who chooses good over evil had not yet been delineated so clearly.

With His argument, Abraham demonstrated that the ethical actions of as few as ten people might be enough to save a whole town. Previous generations knew that if the gods weren't placated through offerings and through the intercession of priests, then famine, pestilence, war, or earthquakes might ensue; but they weren't familiar with the notion that their own moral actions could have a powerful influence. When the Lord said, "For the sake of ten I will not destroy it," the sacred burden of morality was placed squarely on the shoulders of each person. The most humble of individuals—a potter, a shepherd, a mother, a farmer—was assigned a spiritual value equal to that of a priest or king. Each of them now possessed a compelling reason to be obedient to laws of God and behave in an honorable manner: his or her actions *mattered.*

Sodom, as it turns out, does not contain the necessary ten innocent people, a sad fact that condemns it to destruction and transforms it into an enduring reminder of what happens when not enough people are willing to do the right thing.

TESTING A CITY

The test that proves Sodom's communal guilt is provided by two of the three visitors who have been talking with Abraham. The two angels appear at the entrance to Sodom, where Lot welcomes them and invites them to his home so that they can wash their feet and be his guests for the night. When they accept, he prepares a feast and bakes unleavened bread.

As the meal is coming to an end and the guests are preparing to retire for the night, Lot realizes that all the men of Sodom have gathered outside his house, evidently infuriated by the hospitality he has shown to the two strangers. They shout at Lot and demand that he bring the visitors out so that "we may know them." Lot refuses, offering his two virgin daughters instead, but his offer is rejected.

The mob surges forward and begins breaking down the door, but, just as all seems lost, the angels intervene by blinding the men of Sodom so that they cannot find the doorway. The angels warn Lot and his family to leave Sodom because it is going to be destroyed. Lot, his wife, and their two daughters obey, but the fiancés of Lot's daughters laugh at the warning and are left behind.[3]

As the family flees, fire and burning sulfur ("brimstone and fire" in some translations) rain down on Sodom, on the nearby city of

Gomorrah, and on the other cities in the area, "eliminating all life—people, plants, and animals alike." Or, as the Qur'án says, "He destroyed the Overthrown Cities (of Sodom and Gomorrah), so that (ruins unknown) have covered them up."[4]

THE MECHANICS OF DESTRUCTION

The precise locations of Sodom and Gomorrah are still a mystery. One possibility is that cities by that name never existed at all and, instead, the narrative given in the Book of Genesis was based on regional memories of a catastrophic event. Abraham, Moses, and / or one of the writers of the Torah took the memories, reshaped them into a cautionary tale contrasting the good behavior expected of Israelites (represented by the hospitality of Abraham) to the rude conduct of neighboring tribes who did not follow the same religion (i.e., those who were impolite to the visiting angels).

But, if Sodom and Gomorrah did exist during Abraham's lifetime, the words of the Torah indicate that their buildings lay somewhere along the eastern side of the Dead Sea. Several places have been proposed, including Tell el-Hammam, which is currently under excavation, as well as a spot in the south basin of the Dead Sea that is presently covered by water. In either case, the cities were perched tenuously above an earthquake-prone area—the Dead Sea fault—that continues to be active today.[5]

Making the situation even more precarious were the slime pits dotting the land. *Slime pits* sound more gloppy than threatening, but a clearer translation of the original Hebrew word would be *tar pits, puddles of asphalt,* or *pools of bitumen,* any of which can be quite dangerous.*

Asphalt is a natural component of crude oil. It is thick, dark, sticky, and—mixed with sand and stone—makes a very resilient

---

* The problem with using *tar* in translation is that from a chemical point of view, tar and asphalt are different substances. They are both hydrocarbons and have many shared characteristics, but tar is created by the destructive distillation of wood, coal, or peat and softens at a lower temperature than asphalt, which is oil-based.

surface for a highway. Modern refineries generate asphalt as a by-product when they distill crude oil into gasoline, kerosene, and diesel fuel. But, long before any modern refineries were built, Mother Nature was giving mankind access to asphalt in naturally-occurring puddles and ponds. These were created by upwelling arteries of oil bubbling to the surface through layers of sand or cracked rock. After the more volatile gasses and oils had evaporated (a process that could have been speeded up by placing the glop in wicker baskets), the asphalt was ready to use as mortar for laying bricks, glue for mosaics, caulking for boats and roofs, or even to mummify an Egyptian body.[6]

Because crude oil deposits lie beneath so much of the Middle East, tar pits were—and still are—common throughout the region, but other countries have their share, too. Think, for example, of La Brea tar pits in Los Angeles, California; La Brea Del Sur in Venezuela; and the enormous Asphalt Lake of Trinidad.

Four thousand years ago, asphalt was a valuable commodity. Valuable enough to support the growth of several towns—perhaps including Sodom and Gomorrah—whose residents specialized in collecting and trading it. The trade would have generated enough profit to account for the gold and other valuables that had enticed a group of Syrian kings to make war on Sodom soon after Lot moved there (see chapter 9).

Asphalt is not especially flammable after it has dried into a semi-solid mass. But when it is still fairly liquid, before the lighter oils associated with it have evaporated, it can catch fire. So can the methane gas that sometimes bubbles up through liquid asphalt from hidden pockets in the rock below. Combine an earthquake with the explosion of a pocket or two of methane, then add drops of oil flying up into the air and catching fire before gravity brings them down, and it all adds up quite logically to the Torah's descriptions of fire, brimstone, and mass destruction.

Abraham, camped on the higher and safer ground of Mamre, would have been no more than fifty miles away. He rose early in the morning (wakened by a tremor?) and "looked out across the plain to Sodom and Gomorrah and saw columns of smoke and fumes, as from a furnace, rising from the cities there."[7]

THE MANY MEANINGS OF SODOM

A search of the Google Books Web site on March 15, 2011, turned up 23,100 references to books with something to say about the symbolism of Sodom. It is variously seen as a clear-cut mandate to extend hospitality to strangers, a model of the lowest forms of sensory desire, a cautionary tale about the wages of sin, a physical description of the spiritual punishment in store for the wicked, an injunction against homosexuality, a comparison between the way in which the followers of God are expected to act and the way in which unbelievers behave, and a warning about what can happen to believers like Lot who make their home among the unrighteous. It has also been taken as a sign that only those who were physical descendants of Abraham would inherit the blessings of His Covenants with God: In spite of being a faithful believer, Lot was not a direct descendant of Abraham and thus not destined to be the founder of a tribe that would continue to pledge allegiance to the new Revelation.

Another angle from which to view the incident of Sodom and Gomorrah is to understand it as an account of what can happen when a group of people accepts a religion in word but does not adhere to it in deed. From this perspective, the story looks back at history and also forward in prophecy because the same kind of religious hypocrisy has occurred again and again during the last several thousand years. The angelic Messengers represent the religions sent by God—such as the religion of Noah, the religion of Moses, and the religion of Jesus—while Sodom represents those who profess to be followers of these religions. When the angels examine the behavior of the Sodomites, it becomes obvious that although they pretend to be religious, they have been perverting the true intent of their faith. The perversion is indicated by their unnatural lust for the angels—they want to use the angels for their own purposes rather than treat them with honor. When Lot tries to turn the Sodomites away from their perversions (i.e., he offers them the teachings of a new and pure Word of God, symbolized by his two virginal daughters), the men adamantly refuse to change their behavior. They are content with the way they are—disobedient to the old and heedless of the new. Their spiritual blindness means that they cannot see any reason to flee from the wickedness of disobedience, and so their annihilation (physical, spiritual, or both) is inevitable.

A PILLAR OF SALT

Warned by the angels, Lot gathers the members of his family together, and they leave Sodom just before its destruction. Lot's wife, described by Muḥammad as being false to her husband, bitterly resents having to leave the city where she has been happy. She turns and looks back in longing at the wickedness behind her, an act of disloyalty that freezes her into a pillar of salt. The mystical implications of this crystalline image can be explored by examining the ways in which both the helpful and the harmful properties of salt are delineated in scripture.

One of the first passages about salt that springs to mind is Jesus' question: "Ye are the salt of the earth; but if the salt has lost his savour, wherewith shall it be salted?" According to 'Abdu'l-Bahá, Jesus is speaking about the dangers of the "dissensions and lack of unity among His followers," pointing out that if the apostles—the "salt"—are not united, the delicious flavor of the work they do will be lost. There are several other biblical verses that use salt as a metaphor for a quality that is desirable or of value, including this one from Matthew: "Let your speech always be with grace, *as though* seasoned with salt, so that you will know how you should respond to each person."[8]

Muḥammad uses images of salt in several ways, but one of the most intriguing is the manner in which He speaks of the spiritual realm and the material realm as twin oceans. One ocean contains fresh (spiritual) water, while the other is salty. Both oceans yield food and treasure, yet only the fresh water is sweet and pleasant to drink: "He hath let loose the two seas which meet each other . . .

From each he bringeth up pearls both great and small . . . Nor are the two seas alike: the one fresh, sweet, pleasant for drink, and the other salt, bitter; yet from both ye eat fresh fish, and take forth for you ornaments to wear . . ."[9]

Bahá'u'lláh employs the same contrast between fresh and salty to demonstrate the foolishness of rejecting the sweetness of spirituality in favor of the bitterness of materialism: "Yea, inasmuch as the peoples of the world have failed to seek from the luminous and crystal Springs of divine knowledge the inner meaning of God's holy words, they therefore have languished, stricken and sore athirst, in the vale of idle fancy and waywardness. They have strayed far from the fresh and thirst-subduing waters, and gathered round the salt that burneth bitterly."[10]

Applying all these examples from scripture to Lot's wife, she becomes the salt that has lost its savor. She is in disunity with religious truth because she is more attached to the treasures of the salty sea, epitomized by Sodom, than she is to the fresh truths brought by Abraham and preached by her husband. She refuses to drink from the "crystal Springs of divine knowledge" and wishes only to immerse herself in the bitter ocean of physical existence, a wish that causes her to become so encrusted with its sediment that she is spiritually immobilized.

14

DYING OF THIRST

This place is a nowhere of the hill.
Who would stop here so far below the hilltop,
so little above the plain?
This place which all pass by,
I will make my journey's end.
Arthur Shurcliff[1]

As had been promised more than a year earlier, before the destruction of Sodom, Sarah became pregnant. In due time, she delivered a bouncing baby boy. Abraham named the boy *Isaac*, as God previously directed Him to do. Sarah, thrilled at having a baby after so many barren years, exclaimed, "God has brought laughter for me; everyone who hears will laugh with me." This image of delight beautifully expresses the joy of the moment while simultaneously reminding us that *Isaac* means *he will laugh*. Abraham was equally pleased at having another son and a second heir. According to Muḥammad, He rejoiced with these words: "Praise to God who hath bestowed on me, notwithstanding my old age, Ishmael and Isaac!"[2]

Sarah's uncomplicated joy at having a son of her own lasted for a year or even two—until the day Isaac was weaned and Abraham hosted a feast in his honor. During the party, "Sarah saw the son of Hagar the Egyptian, whom she had borne to Abraham, mocking [Isaac]." Furious, Sarah said to Abraham, "Drive out this maid and her son; for the son of this maid shall not be an heir with my son Isaac."[3]

The mocking done by Ishmael is thought to indicate a boast that he, as the firstborn son, stood to inherit more from Abraham than his younger half-brother, a sort of a *Daddy loves me best* taunt. The boast would have been based on the common traditions of inheritance, which gave preference to a firstborn son and allotted him twice as much as a second-born. Sarah, hearing the taunt, would have wanted to protect Isaac and find a way to make sure that he received at least as much as Ishmael. To do this, she would have to invoke her own right, as Abraham's true wife, to claim precedence for her own firstborn son over the firstborn son of the concubine, even though the concubine's son was the elder son. If Abraham sent Hagar and Ishmael away, it would be a clear indication to Hagar and to everyone else that Abraham Himself recognized Sarah's right to claim for Isaac the station of being the primary heir.

Genesis states that Abraham, who loved Ishmael dearly, was distressed by Sarah's request to cast Hagar and Ishmael out. To allay this distress, God said these words to Abraham: "Let it not be grievous in thy sight because of the lad, and because of thy bondwoman; in all that Sarah hath said unto thee, hearken unto her voice; for in Isaac shall thy seed be called. And also of the son of the bondwoman will I make a nation, because he is thy seed."[4]

Hearing these words of comfort, Abraham is assured that Hagar is still slated to receive what she was previously promised: a great nation through Ishmael "because he is thy seed." It also becomes clear at this point that what is happening is a fulfillment of a previous prophecy. When Hagar was first pregnant with Ishmael, the angel of the Lord informed her that Ishmael would live "to the east." So when Sarah asks Abraham to cast Hagar and Ishmael out, she is not really twisting the plot at all. Sarah is fulfilling what was destined from the beginning: Isaac's line will be the one to continue in Canaan, while Ishmael must travel east to claim his rightful place.

The phrase "in Isaac shall thy seed be called" catches the eye because it does not limit Isaac's descendants to one great nation, one great religion, or one great event. *Zera,* the Hebrew word that is translated as *seed,* also implies *posterity* and *sowing-time,* thus imbuing the phrase "in Isaac shall thy seed be called" with the sense of an immense span of time. Indeed, this phrase allows for the possibility of numerous occasions when God might call out to Isaac's posterity and raise a new nation, or sow the seed of a new religion by anointing a new Messenger.

Abraham is, as always, obedient to the command of God: "Early the next morning Abraham took some food and a skin of water and gave them to Hagar. He set them on her shoulders and then sent her off with the boy."[5]

IN THE WILDERNESS

The Old Testament and Muslim hadith agree in substance, though not in every detail, about what happened to Hagar and Ishmael after they left home. Merging the two accounts creates a harrowing tale: Abraham didn't just send Hagar and Ishmael off alone from Canaan; He went along to see the two of them safely to their destination. The trio traveled together until they reached a spot on the southwestern side of the Arabian Peninsula—the very place where the city of Mecca would someday sit.

When they reached the appointed spot, Abraham gave a leather bag of dates to Hagar as well as a skin of water. Bidding her farewell, He turned away and began the long trek back to Canaan, a journey of "forty camel days." Hagar, horrified to be abandoned in such a barren place, chased behind Abraham, pleading with Him, but He refused to stop. Realizing that her words were having no effect, she tried something else. She asked if this was what God had ordered. When Abraham said, "Yes," she said, "Then He will not neglect us.'"[6]

Resigned to her fate, Hagar returned to the spot where Ishmael waited with the water and dates. Abraham, meanwhile, moved steadfastly away until He was out of their sight. Then He stopped, raised His hands and prayed for His concubine and their son: "O our Lord! I have made some of my offspring to dwell in a valley without cultivation . . . in order, O our Lord, that they may establish regular prayer: so fill the hearts of some among men with love towards them, and feed them with Fruits: so that they may give thanks."[7]

Hagar and Ishmael stayed where Abraham had left them until the dates were eaten, the water in the skin was gone, and they were growing weak from thirst. When Hagar could no longer bear to watch her son suffer, she left Ishmael in the shade of a bush. "Then she went off and sat down nearby, about a bowshot away, for she thought, 'I cannot watch the boy die.'"[8]

Hoping to see a person—or a cloud of dust from a caravan—Hagar climbed up the side of the nearest mountain and looked out over the valley, but it was empty. Thinking that things might look better in a different direction, she tucked up her robe and ran back down the mountain, across the valley and up the side of a second mountain. Again, nothing. In increasing desperation, she repeated her run from high point to high point, crossing the valley a total of seven times.

Then "She heard a voice and she asked herself to be quiet and listened attentively. She heard the voice again and said, 'O, (whoever you may be)! You have made me hear your voice; have you got something to help me?' And behold! She saw an angel . . . digging the earth . . . till water flowed from that place." The spring gushed so freely that Hagar feared it might soon exhaust itself, so she began muttering "Zomë Zomë" or "stop flowing" while she scooped out a basin to keep the liquid from being lost in the desert sand. The name of the spring—ZamZam—is said to have come from those words. And its location marked the area where the city of Mecca (also known as *Becca, Baca,* or *Bakkah)* would someday stand.[9]

Hagar and Ishmael were revived by the water and reassured by a final repetition of God's promise. The angel of God then spoke to Hagar, saying, "What aileth thee, Hagar? fear not; for God hath heard the voice of the lad where he is. Arise, lift up the lad, and hold him in thine hand; for I will make him a great nation."[10]

Hagar and Ishmael settled into their new life, and "God was with the lad; and he grew, and dwelt in the wilderness, and became an archer. And he dwelt in the wilderness of Paran."[11]

The struggle faced by Hagar and Ishmael in adapting to a harsh life in a new land can be understood on at least three levels of mystical meaning.

First, it can be read as a parable about the growth of Hagar's spiritual understanding. Hagar came from Egypt and from a polytheistic background. She had been given, perhaps against her will, to Sarah for a servant, and there is no indication that she had understood Abraham's position in the same way Sarah did. Yes, she returned after her attempt at running away, but she continued to behave badly by letting—or perhaps even encouraging—her son to mock Isaac. Only when she was ejected from Canaan and left to die of thirst in a wilderness—a nice metaphor for being spiritually confused—did she completely come to terms with her own need for a reviving draught of the water of life.

On a second level, the designation of Ishmael as an *archer* can be understood to mean that he was a saintly man who was able to shoot "sure arrows of knowledge" that affected the hearts of those who lived in the wilderness of ignorance. The Qur'án reinforces this understanding of Ishmael's spirituality by describing him as an admirable apostle who "used to enjoin on his people Prayer and Charity, and he was most acceptable in the sight of his Lord."[12]

Third, the way that Hagar and Ishmael settled in "the wilderness of Paran" is seen by Islam and the Bahá'í Faith as a prophecy about Arabia and the advent of Muḥammad. This is because Paran was a town along the northwestern border of Arabia, and thus any mention of it can be taken to indicate the whole of Arabia, much as the term *Ur of the Chaldees* was used to designate a much wider area than the city of Ur itself.[13]

THE FIRST HOUSE OF WORSHIP

In checking the Qur'án, the Muslim hadith, and other historical sources, one discovers that Abraham did not forget about Hagar and Ishmael after they settled in their new home. He returned to visit them at least once, and maybe as many as four times. During one of these visits, Abraham and Ishmael were directed to a site, close to the well of Zamzam, where God wanted them to erect a sanctuary. The directions for building it were quite precise. It was to be in the form of a cube and oriented so that the four corners were in line with the four points of a compass: north, east, south, and west.

Abraham and Ishmael were also directed to put something inside the sanctuary—an undistinguished rock about twelve inches in diameter that was placed at the eastern corner, perhaps to mark the direction to which one should turn in prayer, perhaps as a symbol of abandoning carved idols, or perhaps to mark this as the "east" where Ishmael would live and Muḥammad, his descendant, would be born. The sanctuary was called the *Kaaba*—the *cube*—and it became a holy site of pilgrimage for those who continued to remember Abraham, a group that included Ishmael's children and grandchildren as well as their cousins, the Jewish descendants of Isaac.[14]

The sanctuary of the Kaaba and the events associated with it are so sacred to religious history that King David apparently speaks of them in the Book of Psalms, describing the way in which Abraham found a home where Hagar could build a nest for her son. He gives special pathos to the verses by a clever play on words; he substitutes a homophone—*Baca*—for the name of the town in which Hagar settled (Mecca was then known as *Becca* or *Bakkah*). Because *Baca* means *Valley of Weeping* or *Valley of Lamentation*, it evokes the memory of Hagar's bitter tears in a way that the straight use of *Becca* or *Bakkah* could never do. David also seems to look both behind and ahead when he says that those who pass though the valley (i.e. Abraham and, later, Muḥammad) make springs of water—divine and physical—begin to flow. Here are the verses:

Even the sparrow has found a home,
And the swallow a nest for herself
Where she may have her young—
A place near your altar,
O Lord Almighty, my King and my God.
Blessed are those who dwell in your house;
They are ever praising you.
Blessed are those whose strength is in you,
Who have set their hearts on pilgrimage.
As they pass through the Valley of Baca,
They make it a place of springs.[15]

Muḥammad reconfirmed the sacredness of the Kaaba in the Qur'án with this description: "The first temple that was founded for mankind, was that in Becca, Blessed, and a guidance to human beings. In it are evident signs, even the standing-place of Abraham: and he who entereth it is safe."[16]

After the passing of Abraham and Ishmael, monotheism—or at least some version of the faith that Abraham had modeled—was practiced by many of the people who lived near the Kaaba. When the descendants of Ishmael became so numerous that the Valley of Weeping began to feel crowded, those who moved away often grabbed a stone from the area around the Kaaba and took it along to use as a foundation for erecting a place of worship in their new homes. Alas, the true meaning of the stones and of the original sanctuary was lost as information was passed from generation to generation. Slowly but steadily, the worship of a single God degenerated into the polytheistic worship of various tribal gods and goddesses, and those who still visited the Kaaba often desecrated it by littering the area with their favorite idols. Even the spring of ZamZam, whose slightly brackish liquid had eased the dusty throats of thousands of pilgrims, was abandoned in favor of fresher-tasting water from newer wells in other parts of the city. Sand blew in, covering the wellspring opening, and after a while, no one could remember exactly where ZamZam had been. Nor did they care.[17]

"God's gift was no longer a necessity, and the Holy Well became a half-forgotten memory" until Muḥammad's grandfather was led, by means of a dream, to rediscover it. A few years later, in AD 630, Muḥammad boldly destroyed all of the idols around the Kaaba— said to number three hundred and sixty—and had the structure cleaned and repaired. He also designated the rock inside the Kaaba as the *Qib'lih* or *point of adoration* to which Muslims should turn during prayer. Five times a day, millions of faithful Muslims around the world still bow their heads toward the rock once touched by the hands of Abraham.[18]

15

THE MYSTERY OF SACRIFICE

Was not our ancestor Abraham
considered righteous for what he did
when he offered his son . . . on the altar?
You see that his faith and his actions were working together,
and his faith was made complete by what he did.

James[1]

With Isaac growing up in Canaan and Ishmael established in
Arabia, life ought to have been quiet for Abraham, but it wasn't.
God commanded Him to "Take your son, your only son, whom
you love . . . and go to the land of Moriah. Sacrifice him there as a
burnt offering on one of the mountains . . ."[2]

Two questions immediately arise on reading these alarming sen-
tences: Which son was the "only son," and what was the purpose of
such a strange sacrifice?

WHICH SON?

According to the text of Genesis, Isaac was the one to be
sacrificed. This statement has caused much confusion because it
was impossible for Isaac to be Abraham's *only son*. There was just
one child who could have been the *only*, and that would have been
Ishmael in the years before Isaac was born.

The mystery continued even after the coming of Jesus because He never mentioned the sacrificial victim by name. The only identification was done by one of the apostles—James—who simply echoed the Genesis text in identifying the son as Isaac.

The first hint of a solution to the quandary occurred when Muḥammad, as quoted in the Qur'án, strongly hinted that Ishmael was the sacrificial son and implied that the incident took place before the birth of Isaac, during the period of time when Ishmael truly was "the only son." Bahá'u'lláh later confirmed Muḥammad's hint by directly identifying Ishmael as the one who was to be offered up.[3]

The corrections given by Muḥammad and Bahá'u'lláh to the account in Genesis make it clear that, for whatever reason, the version of the sacrifice given in Genesis is not perfect. We don't know why Jesus didn't mention and correct the error, but He might have realized that His followers were not yet ready to appreciate Ishmael's rightful place in the Abrahamic drama. Perhaps the true identity of the *only son* was part of what Jesus referred to when He said, "I have yet many things to say unto you, but ye cannot bear them now." Another possibility is that Jesus wanted His followers to come to the realization all by themselves that, from a spiritual point of view, the name of the sacrificial son has never been essential to the story because the pivotal point of the incident is not the child's identity but the fact that Abraham was willing to obey God's command.[4]

WHY?

The thought of killing one's child, even if called by God to do so, is so repugnant to most of us that this incident has caused more outrage, confusion, anger, and sorrow in human hearts than any other part of Abraham's life. Contemporary eyes view this as "a horrible story; it depicts God as a despotic and capricious sadist, and it is not surprising that many people today who have heard this tale as children reject such a deity."[5] Getting beyond the horror requires a serious study of the mystery of sacrifice, especially as it pertains to the life of a Messenger of God.

By all accounts, it is dauntingly difficult to come to terms with accepting the station of being a Manifestation of God. The first challenge every Messenger faces is to sacrifice His own wants. He must willingly surrender any hope of experiencing the pleasures of a normal life and accept all of the difficulties inherent in announcing a new Revelation from God. He knows from the beginning that He will face constant harassment and that He may be tortured, jailed, reviled, spat upon, or killed.

The Báb, recounting His own moment of realizing what fate had in store, said, "I heard a Voice calling in my inmost being: 'Do thou sacrifice the thing which Thou lovest most in the path of God . . .'" Jesus, when He was anointed by the Holy Spirit, spent forty days in the wilderness wrestling with the knowledge of what would befall Him as soon as He began preaching a new doctrine. Bahá'u'lláh, Who retreated to the remote uplands of Kurdistan for two years before announcing His Revelation, vividly described the way in which He, too, was overcome with tumultuous emotions: "From Our eyes there rained tears of anguish, and in Our bleeding heart surged an ocean of agonizing pain."[6]

When, in spite of knowing the price He will pay, a Messenger embraces the future, He does so out of devotion to God and because He feels an overwhelming love for mankind. He understands that His self-sacrifice has the power to ignite a torch of spirituality that will illumine the souls of those who are ready to accept a new message from God and, through them, change the world: "This is the reason why the universal Manifestations of God unveil Their countenances to man, and endure every calamity and sore affliction, and lay down Their lives as a ransom; it is to make these very people, the ready ones, the ones who have capacity, to become dawning points of light, and to bestow upon them the life that fadeth never. This is the true sacrifice: the offering of oneself, even as did Christ, as a ransom for the life of the world."[7]

The sacrifices made by Messengers of God can be startling and even terrifying, but they are also illuminating and inspiring. The calm and loving manner in which They bear the sufferings heaped upon Them brilliantly demonstrates the eternal nature of the soul. "If the spirit were not immortal," 'Abdu'l-Bahá asks, "how could the Manifestations of God endure such terrible trials? Why did Christ Jesus suffer the fearful death on the cross? Why did Muḥammad bear persecutions? Why did the Báb make the supreme sacrifice and why did Bahá'u'lláh pass the years of his life in prison? Why should all this suffering have been, if not to prove the everlasting life of the spirit?"[8]

Oddly, it is a children's book whose pages hold one of the simplest and most beautiful portrayals of the mystical power of this kind of sacrifice. In C. S. Lewis' book, *The Lion, The Witch and the Wardrobe*, Aslan, an honorable and very powerful lion, humbly offers to take the place of a boy named Edmund. The boy has been condemned because, according to the law of the country of Narnia, he has forfeited his own life by betraying his siblings. The wicked witch-queen of the story, who loathes the nobility of the lion, accepts the trade. After her minions bind Aslan to a stone table, she raises her killing knife with rampant glee.

According to the witch's view of the world, killing Aslan instead of Edmund will do two marvelous things: It will appease the Deep Magic—the law of the land—which requires atonement for Edmund's betrayal. Even better, it will get rid of her primary rival, Aslan, and make her the most powerful person in Narnia. Then, as soon as Aslan is dead, she will be able to renege on the original agreement and have the delicious pleasure of killing Edmund anyway.

Before the knife plunges into Aslan's heart, the witch-queen taunts him with a grim prediction: "Understand that you have given me Narnia forever, you have lost your own life and you have not saved his. In that knowledge, despair and die." The lion remains calm, the knife strikes, Aslan dies, the stone table on which he is lying cracks in half, and those who love him weep despairingly.

The next day, to everyone's astonishment, the lion reappears in full and living glory. This is possible, he explains, because although "the Witch knew the Deep Magic, there is a magic deeper still which she did not know. Her knowledge goes back only to the dawn of time. But if she could have looked a little further back, into the stillness and the darkness before Time dawned, she would have read there a different incantation. She would have known that when a willing victim who had committed no treachery was killed in a traitor's stead, the Table would crack and Death itself would start working backward."[9]

In contemplating the implications of *magic deeper still* (the spiritual laws undergirding the physical laws of the universe), the sacrifice of Ishmael reveals itself as a more significant act than Abraham's offering of His own life would have been because—as any loving parent knows—it is far easier to think of killing oneself than one's child. The potential power of the sacrifice was further increased by the fact that, according to Muḥammad, Ishmael was a willing partner in the whole thing. As soon as Abraham mentioned what God had commanded, Ishmael acquiesced, saying, "do what thou art bidden."[10]

With not one but two sacrifices involved—Abraham surrendering the objections of His heart and Ishmael giving up his body—the recompense designated by God must have been exceedingly special. And it was. The purpose of God, Bahá'u'lláh explains, was to sacrifice Ishmael "as a ransom for the sins and iniquities of all the peoples of the earth."[11]

THE RANSOM

On the morning after God had requested the sacrifice of Abraham's only son, Ishmael and Abraham rose early. Calling for two servants to accompany them, Abraham saddled a donkey, and the party of four began a three-day trek toward the mountain where the burnt offering would be made As they drew near their destination, Abraham told the servants to hunker down, keep an eye on the donkey, and wait for His return. Abraham had brought a load of wood along, and He now loaded it onto the strong shoulders of Ishmael. When that was done, Abraham picked up a knife, grabbed a firepot with which to kindle the wood, and the two of them walked out of sight.

Following the plan He had been given, Abraham built an altar and placed the wood on it. He laid Ishmael on the wood so that he was in the proper position to be burned. Gripping the knife, He prepared to slay His cherished son before lighting the fire that would consume the dead body. Then something unexpected happened: "But the angel of the Lord called to him from heaven and said, 'Abraham! Abraham!' And he said, 'Here I am.'"[12]

The Old Testament, the Qur'án, and the Bahá'í scriptures all confirm that God halted Abraham's hand and prevented Him from killing His son. They also agree that in lieu of the son, something else was sacrificed. The Old Testament describes the substitute as a ram, saying, "Abraham lifted up his eyes, and looked, and behold behind him a ram caught in a thicket by his horns: and Abraham went and took the ram, and offered him up for a burnt offering in the stead of his son."[13]

A few hundred years later, during the Revelation of Moses, the basic scenario of substituting an animal for a child was repeated. When the Angel of Death was called by God to pass over Egypt and kill all firstborn sons, including the infant son of Moses and the sons of His followers, Moses instructed each family to sacrifice a lamb. Blood from the lambs was used to mark the doorposts of the faithful families so that the Angel would know to pass over those houses and spare the babies within.

In considering the many spiritual functions of the ram / lamb in the sacrifices made by Abraham and Moses, two possibilities leap out immediately: an educational function and a prophetic one.

The act of sacrifice itself was nothing new because cultures around the world had been accustomed to sacrificing an animal or a person long before Abraham and Moses arrived on the scene. When a sacrifice was made—including a human sacrifice—eating some vital part of the victim was sometimes part of the ritual. Because human sacrifice was still being practiced in Canaan and other regions during the lifetimes of both Abraham and Moses, it is logical to conclude that one of the goals of these Messengers of

God was to bring an end to this spiritually degrading practice. The tribes of that period might not have been ready to totally dispense with the ritual of sacrificing something living, but by dramatically substituting an animal for a child and showing that God approved of the substitution, Moses and Abraham were able to make a little progress. By demonstrating that it was more pleasing to God to kill an animal than a person, They allowed Their followers to practice a satisfactorily tangible method of sacrifice while simultaneously stressing the sacredness of human life.

The prophetic purpose of the animal sacrifices made by Abraham and Moses could have been that of getting mankind ready for vital spiritual lesson to be taught by future religions: self-sacrifice is even more potent than animal sacrifice.

How Many Lambs?

In the coming centuries, several of Abraham's descendants would step forward to teach the lesson of self-sacrifice by becoming the ram, becoming the lamb, becoming a voluntary substitute for Ishmael and demonstrating the redeeming power of self-sacrifice.

In Christianity, Jesus sacrificed Himself. Soon after John the Baptist met Jesus, he showed that he understood the relationship between Jesus and the ram / lamb by proclaiming "Behold the Lamb of God, which taketh away the sin of the world." After Jesus had been crucified c. AD 29, the Apostle Peter reinforced the symbolic connection between Jesus and the sacrificed ram by saying that Jesus had redeemed mankind "with the precious blood of Christ, as of a lamb without blemish and without spot."[14]

Many of Jesus' early followers absorbed His lesson about the power of self-sacrifice so completely that they continued to tell others about the new religion even when threatened with torture or death. Martyrs like St. Stephen, who was stoned to death, and St. Peter, who was crucified by Nero, come immediately to mind. But, powerful as these examples were, not everyone managed to learn the lesson. Ritual animal sacrifice continued to be the norm in dozens of cultures while the example of spiritual self-sacrifice and restraint embedded in Jesus' teaching of "turn the other cheek" was often ignored.

In Islam, the lesson about self-sacrifice was taught by the Imam Ḥusayn, a grandson of Muḥammad. Ḥusayn was the third Imam (spiritual leader) of Shia Islam, and his greatest desire was to turn the young religion of Islam away from the wayward path it had begun to follow under the direction of the Umayyad clan that had seized power after the death of Muḥammad's son-in-law, 'Alí.

When Ḥusayn refused to acknowledge the supremacy of the new Umayyad ruler, Caliph Yazid I—an alcoholic who openly flouted many of the laws given by Muḥammad—he knew that the act would result in his own death. In AD 680, while returning from Mecca to his home in Kufa, Ḥusayn and a group of about seventy friends and family members were confronted by an army of four thousand men who demanded he sign a pledge of allegiance to Yazid. When Ḥusayn refused, his group was slaughtered, except for the women and most of the children. The dead men were decapitated and their heads raised on spears by the triumphant troops.

The horror of these brutal acts and the unwarranted death of Muḥammad's beloved grandson created an upwelling of protest that ultimately led to a revolt against the Umayyad dynasty. In AD 750, the dynasty—and its interpretation of Islam—was overthrown. Some historians have concluded that because of Ḥusayn's sacrifice, Islam became a more thoughtful and morally conscious religion than it might otherwise have been. Shia Muslims continue to commemorate the death of the Imam Ḥusayn each year with a ten-day period of mourning.[15]

The sacrificial lamb of the Bábí Faith was the Báb Himself. Like Jesus, the Báb's period of ministry was very short—just six years. He was only thirty when, in 1850, He was put to death by a firing squad of seven hundred and fifty men in Tabriz, Iran. In the wake of His death, hundreds of recent converts followed His example by allowing themselves to be tortured or killed rather than renounce their new faith.[16]

In the Bahá'í Faith, one could cite any number of people who have been martyred in the years since Bahá'u'lláh died, sacrificing their lives as willingly as the ram / lamb. One of the most poignant examples, however, lies in the way that Mírzá Mihdí, the youngest son of Bahá'u'lláh, offered his own life as a ransom with a specific purpose.

Mírzá Mihdí was, with other members of Bahá'u'lláh's family, imprisoned in the fetid prison of Acre after having been exiled from Turkey in 1868. Like many other buildings of that period, the roof of the prison was flat and dotted with unguarded holes serving as skylights for the floor below. Mírzá Mihdí, who liked to climb up to the flat roof in the evening so that he could pace back and forth while saying prayers, lost his footing and fell through one of the holes. He landed on a wooden crate, and one of its boards pierced his chest. Bahá'u'lláh heard the crash and rushed to the scene. Because Bahá'u'lláh was a Messenger of God, it is assumed that He could have chosen to save the life of His son, but when He asked Mírzá Mihdí if he wished to live, the answer was extraordinary. Mírzá Mihdí explained that he wanted his life to be accepted as a ransom for all of the pilgrims who had traveled great distances to visit Bahá'u'lláh but were denied the privilege of seeing Him. "God will grant your wish," Bahá'u'lláh replied.[17]

Mírzá Mihdí died the next day, on June 23, 1870, at the age of twenty-two. Three months later, the government abruptly decided to use the prison as barracks for troops. To make this possible, it opened the doors of the prison and provided much more pleasant housing for the inmates elsewhere. With this change, the government inadvertently began allowing Bahá'u'lláh to receive visitors, thus fulfilling Mírzá Mihdí's wish that pilgrims be given access to his Father. Through the ever-enlarging procession of visitors, information about the Bahá'í Faith began to spread out into the world in a way that would have been impossible had Bahá'u'lláh remained in the prison building.

In one of Bahá'u'lláh's prayers, He speaks of Mírzá Mihdí with great tenderness and promises that his dying wish will be granted, saying, "Thou art the Trust of God and His Treasure in this Land. Erelong will God reveal through thee that which He hath desired." The prayer also contains a sentence sharp enough to wound the heart of every bereaved parent, a sentence that could just as easily have been said by Abraham, by Joseph, father of Jesus; by Muḥammad, the grandfather of Ḥusayn; or by the Báb: *"I have, O my Lord, offered up that which Thou hast given Me, that Thy servants may be quickened, and all that dwell on earth be united."*[18]

16

A FINAL RESTING PLACE

Thus thou shalt plant a garden round the tomb,
Where golden hopes may flower, and fruits immortal bloom.
James D. Burns[1]

Sarah was younger than Abraham, but she died before He did. She had traveled a long way with her husband, had been faithful to His cause, had been instrumental in giving Him a child by Hagar, and then had given birth to a son of her own whose descendants would be extremely important to humanity. She was, 'Abdu'l-Bahá notes, a woman who "glorified the human race" by her excellence, and Abraham mourned her passing.[2]

Sarah died in Mamre, a couple of miles outside the village of Hebron, which is about twenty-five miles south of Jerusalem. Hebron was controlled by a local Canaanite tribe that seems to have been indifferent to the presence of Abraham—neither hostile nor particularly welcoming. They might have had respect for Abraham, but He was clearly not part of their society and held no status in their eyes as a Messenger of God. He was just a humble sojourner, a resident alien Who lived in a tent and herded sheep that dined on wild grasses. When it came to burying a wife who was also a foreigner, Abraham would have been expected to follow the usual custom of using either a pit or a cave to hold the body.

If Abraham were to dig a shallow pit, it might be in an informal community cemetery already established to hold family members and servants that had been part of the extended households of Abraham and Lot. Each pit in the cemetery would probably have been lined with flat chunks of rock and topped off with a heavy slab of stone plus a heap of boulders. A large pottery jar, of the kind used to store grain or oil, might have been placed on top as a marker. An alternative method of burial, also in common use, would have been to find a cave on a rocky hillside in the wilderness and use it as family tomb where Abraham, too, when the time came, could be laid to rest beside Sarah.

But, in what must have been a surprising move to those around Him, Abraham did neither of these things. Instead, He went into the town of Hebron.

Abraham approached the elders of the town and bowed before them in greeting, saying, "I am a sojourning settler with you. Grant me a burial holding with you, and let me bury my dead now before me." The men welcomed Abraham with perfunctory courtesy, but they ignored the idea of His buying any of the land lying within their control, probably because the notion of selling to an outsider would have been repugnant. They suggested, instead, that He choose one of the existing tombs in Hebron, promising that "none of us will refuse you his grave for burying your dead." [3]

Community and family tombs—caves or excavations that could hold multiple bodies—were common throughout Canaan. The elders might well have assumed that before Sarah was placed in one of the tombs, her body would spend several months in a shallow hillside pit where it could decompose. After that, the burial in Hebron would be a simple matter of gathering her bones and putting them in a box or jar. The jar would subsequently be placed in one of the existing tombs, where it would occupy very little space. [4]

Abraham bowed once again to the elders to show His respect and then deftly used their offer as a means of turning the conversation in the direction He intended it to go. "If you are willing to let me bury my dead," He said, "Intercede with Ephron, son of Zoar, on my behalf so he will sell me the cave of Machpelah, which belongs to him and is at the end of his field."[5]

The cave of Machpelah lay at the outer edge of the town, near Mamre, a location that would have made its sale at least marginally palatable to the townsmen because Abraham could approach it without walking across any of the property that already belonged to Hebron's other residents. And, enticingly, Abraham also announced that He wasn't looking for a bargain: "Ask him to sell it to me for the full price as a burial site among you."[6]

Ephron, who had been sitting quietly among the elders, heard every word—as Abraham undoubtedly intended. He refused to take any money but offered the cave, along with the surrounding field, as a gift to Abraham, though in a manner that may have been contemptuous and clearly was not meant to be taken seriously. "I will give you the cave and the field. Here in the presence of my people, I give it to you. Go and bury your dead."[7]

Abraham, naturally, declined the spurious offer. But He pounced on the fact that Ephron had linked land and cave and made them a package deal. "I will give the price of the field," Abraham said, and "accept it from me that I may bury my dead there."[8] The tenor of the text of Genesis indicates that buying both land and cave was really what Abraham had intended all along, but that He had been wise enough to ask only for the cave at the beginning and let the first hint of selling the land come from the mouth of the owner.

Ephron, whether through greed at being able to name a price without any bargaining or from scornful glee at the chance to publicly humiliate an outsider, demanded an exorbitant sum: "Well, the land is worth four hundred pieces of silver but what is that between friends?"[9]

Abraham now had exactly what He needed, though at the outset it had seemed impossible—the offer of land and an appropriate cave in Hebron for a price determined by the owner and witnessed by the city elders. And, high though the price was, He had come prepared to pay it.

At this point, Ephron faced the prospect of concluding the deal or losing face in front of his peers. And because Abraham was paying exactly what was asked, with none of the usual bargaining to lower the price, Ephron and the rest of the townspeople would never be able to claim at a later date that a fair price had not been paid: "So Ephron's field, which was in Machpelah, which faced Mamre, the field and cave which was in it, and all the trees which were in the field, that were within all the confines of its border, were deeded over to Abraham for a possession."[10]

Machpelah means *two caves* or *double caves*, but that shouldn't necessarily be taken as indicating huge underground caverns. A traditional burial cave in Canaan, whether natural or man-made, was often quite small, maybe the size of a small bathroom. It was connected to the surface of the earth by a vertical shaft or a horizontal passageway through which someone could carry a body or jar of bones. After entombment, the entrance to the cave would be sealed with a boulder or slab of rock. Stones, rubble, and earth would be thrown into the shaft, filling it and rising in a mound to mark the location. For a second interment, the mound would be removed and the shaft cleared out so that the tomb could be reentered.

When Abraham died, He was entombed in the cave of Machpelah with Sarah. Because Abraham had bought the land outright, as a permanent family burial place, Isaac inherited the rights to it and was also buried there, as was his wife, Rebekah. The body of Isaac's son, Jacob, was mummified in Egypt, where he had been living, and it was carried back to Canaan so that he could also be placed in the tomb alongside the remains of his first wife, Leah. A few traditions say that Ishmael was buried in the tomb as well, but that seems unlikely.

As the number of people who believed in Abraham grew, so did the honor accorded the tomb. Hebron itself, located along one of the trade routes between Egypt and Mesopotamia, also grew, expanding from a small settlement into an important city. After the advent of Moses and the return of the Israelites, Jews flocked to the city as pilgrims, and many sought to be buried near the tomb, all of which added to the city's renown. In 1000 BC, David was crowned king there and made it his capital. Later on, about a hundred years before the birth of Jesus, a nine-foot-thick wall of chiseled stone blocks was built around the site, and the ruins of these walls still stand.

After the Romans invaded Palestine and sacked Jerusalem in AD 70, many Jews fled to other countries, but a small group remained in Hebron with the specific intent of caring for the tomb. When Christianity became the official religion of the Roman Empire, Jews were supplanted by Christians as official caretakers. Christians, who regarded Abraham as a forefather and revered Him as a saint, were vigilant in their protection of the site. They built a roof over the walls, enclosing the area, and used it as a church, though Jews were still given at least occasional access to the tombs. When a formal basilica was built above the tombs in the sixth century, the custom of allowing Jewish access was continued, and Jews were also allowed to worship in a special section of the building.[11]

Christian occupancy yielded to Muslim rule in AD 678 when a Muslim army took control of Hebron. Muslims, like Jews and Christians, venerated Abraham, and they continued the tradition of taking great care of the site. They converted the Christian basilica into the Mosque of Ibrahim, but it was reconverted to a church when Christian Crusaders successfully invaded in AD 1100. Eighty-seven years later, Muslims regained control, and they have maintained ownership of most of the site since then, although a Jewish area with a small synagogue still exists at the north side of the shrine area.

In spite of the fact that the followers of Judaism, Christianity, and Islam have not always gotten along well together, their shared respect for the tomb bought so carefully by Abraham has made it one of the oldest (perhaps *the* oldest) continually cared-for religious sites on earth. Its presence in the world today is a potent reminder of the enduring strength of the promises made to Abraham's descendants.

17

THREE WEDDINGS AND A FUNERAL

And when He desired to manifest grace and beneficence to men,
and to set the world in order,
He revealed observances and created laws;
among them He established the law of marriage,
made it as a fortress for well-being and salvation,
and enjoined it upon us in that which was sent down
out of the heaven of sanctity in His Most Holy Book.
Bahá'u'lláh[1]

REBEKAH

To comfort Isaac after his mother's death, Abraham decided to obtain a wife for him. Any woman who planned to become Isaac's wife would have to leave her own home and join him in Canaan because Abraham did not want Isaac to leave the land God had promised to give to His descendants.

What's more, Abraham wanted a relative rather than a Canaanite to be Isaac's wife. So, to find the perfect mate, Abraham called upon a highly-trusted servant, asking him to travel all the way "to my homeland, to my relatives, and find a wife there for my son Isaac."[2]

The servant (presumed but not proven to be Abraham's chief steward, Eliezar), "took ten of his master's camels and departed, taking all kinds of choice gifts from his master; and he set out and went to Aram-naharaim, to the city of Nahor."³ The *city of Nahor* named in Genesis was, almost certainly, the town of Harran—the place where the family and descendants of Abraham's brother, Nahor, were living. Nahor had married Milcah, who was the daughter of Abraham's youngest brother, Harran—the brother who died in Ur before the rest of the family was exiled from Ur to Harran. Milcah had subsequently given birth to eight children, and she and Nahor now had grandchildren as well, creating a large extended family from which a bride could be chosen.

When Eliezar arrived in Harran, the blazing afternoon sun was fading, and dusk was approaching. Many of the women of the town were gathered at the town's primary well, obtaining water with which to replenish the containers at their homes.

Fully aware of the importance of finding the right wife for Isaac, a wife who would be kind and generous of spirit, Eliezar prayed for success: "Let the girl to whom I shall say, 'Please offer your jar that I may drink,' and who shall say, 'Drink, and I will water your camels'—let her be the one whom you have appointed for your servant Isaac. By this I shall know that you have shown steadfast love to my master."⁴

An offer to draw water from the well for a visitor plus the visitor's camels would be more than a small favor. It would be an act of palpable generosity because the well at Harran was not an easily-accessible fountain or pool. Nor was it a simple hole in the ground with a bucket and rope. It was an underground spring that could only be approached by means of an inclined shaft. To get water, a woman had to walk down the slope, fill her jug and then walk back up again. Water weighs more than eight pounds a gallon, and a water jug of that period might hold three gallons, creating about twenty-five pounds of dead weight to be carried up the slope from the well on each trip, not to mention the additional weight of a two-handled ceramic jug.⁵

Finishing his prayer, Eliezar approached Rebekah and said, "Please give me a little water from your jar."⁶

"Drink, my lord," Rebekah replied, and she "quickly lowered the jar to her hands and gave him a drink. After she had given him a drink, she said, 'I'll draw water for your camels too, until they have finished drinking.' So she quickly emptied her jar into the trough, ran back to the well to draw more water, and drew enough for all his camels."[7]

When the thirst of the camels was slaked, Eliezar took out three of the gifts that Abraham had provided: two gold bracelets and a gold nose ring. Judging by jewelry found nearby excavations, the ornaments were finely-crafted and decorated with lacy patterns of diminutive gold balls.[8]

Rebekah accepted the gifts, and when Eliezar asked if her house had room for him to spend the night, she cordially agreed: "We have plenty of both straw and feed, and a room to lodge in."[9]

After Eliezar followed Rebekah home, he met with her father, Bethuel, and her brother, Laban, and explained his quest. They agreed that Rebekah could return to Canaan with Eliezar and marry Isaac. Then, in a move unusual at that time, they gave Rebekah the honor of deciding for herself whether or not she wanted to proceed with the marriage. She agreed and accompanied Eliezar to Canaan. Isaac was charmed and comforted by his bride, and everything was copacetic.

In the Book of Genesis, the whole bride-seeking adventure is written out in scrupulous detail. It is true that a wife for Isaac was imperative, but the account takes up so much space—more than all three of Abraham's marriages—that one can't help pondering the possibility of numerous mystical layers.

When Rebekah leaves Harran and her family to join Isaac and Abraham, she reunites a family that was torn apart when Abraham announced His new beliefs. Unlike her grandfather, Nahor, who did not join Abraham in exile, Rebekah is willing to journey to a strange land and follow Abraham's teachings. Because she is Abraham's great-niece as well as His daughter-in-law, she reinforces the bloodline and will play an important role in continuing His legacy. Her good character, plus the way in which she independently agrees to marry Isaac, also creates a model for how women should be treated (with respect) and how they should behave (with dignity, thoughtfulness, and generosity).

In many ways, Rebekah is to Isaac what Sarah was to Abraham. The account of her life establishes this relationship by presenting several events that are identical—or nearly so—to those of Sarah's life: Most strikingly, Rebekah is asked by her husband to say she is his sister rather than his wife. This is the very thing that happened twice to Sarah—once in Egypt and again during a visit to an area ruled by Abimelech. Another similarity occurs when Rebekah endures years of being barren before she is able to conceive a child. Furthermore, as Rebekah's children grow up, she realizes that she must help the younger son claim for himself what would normally be the rights of the elder son—reminiscent of the way in which Sarah had to clarify Isaac's position so that he, rather than Ishmael, the firstborn, would be Abraham's primary heir.

On reading the relevant verses in Genesis about Sarah and Rebekah, one wonders how and why the parallels between the two women occurred. Are they a literal recitation of facts or—more likely—are they symbols of certain moral truths? Does the repetition exist precisely so that we will ponder the inner meanings of the stories? Is it possible the events are intended to demonstrate that women are just as important to the history of religion as men are? And does the yielding of an older son to a younger one represent the way in which an older, well-established religion is destined to be upset by a newer and younger Revelation from God?

A Proper Wife for Ishmael

Isaac was not the only brother to marry. Ishmael was also in need of a wife in order to continue his line and fulfill the promises made about his descendants. According to the Torah, Ishmael's wife was selected by his mother, Hagar. She chose a woman from Egypt, presumably because she herself was originally from that country and wanted a daughter-in-law whose customs would be comfortingly similar to her own.

Jewish tradition fleshes out the bare bones scriptural account of Ishmael's wife with a great many details, which are fascinating though not necessarily reliable. According to some accounts, Abraham decided to visit Ishmael in order to meet his wife. When Abraham arrived, Ishmael and Hagar were out collecting dates and pomegranates, but Ishmael's wife was with the children. Abraham greeted the woman and tried to talk with her, but she rebuffed His overtures and refused to give Him any water to quench His thirst. After telling Abraham to leave, she turned her back, entered her tent and began quarreling with her children, cursing them in a loud voice and hitting them as well. Abraham called out to her and asked if she would do him the great favor of giving Ishmael a message.

"Speak, old man," said the wife, who did not guess who Abraham really was, "I am listening unto thee."

"When Ishmael, thy husband, returneth home, tell him this: an old man from the land of Canaan was here and inquired after thee; he also bade thee change the peg of thy tent, for it is a bad one, and to put a better one in its place."

When Ishmael returned to his wife and heard the message, he realized that his father had been to see him and had not been pleased with his wife. Heeding the advice that had been so obliquely tendered, he changed the "peg of his tent" by sending his wife back to her original family and taking a new wife by the name of Fatima. After three years, Abraham visited for the second time, and this time His reception was quite different. When Abraham asked about Ishmael, Fatima replied, "He is away from home, hunting; but prithee, my Lord, come down from thy camel and honour me with thy presence in our humble tent. Rest awhile from the fatigue of thy journey and refresh thyself with food and drink. Thou wilt thus bestow a great favour upon thy servant."

Abraham accepted Fatima's hospitality and stayed long enough to pray with her and share a meal. As they parted, Abraham asked

Fatima to tell Ishmael that an old man "bade me say that he found the new peg of thy tent a very good one. He bade thee keep it and cherish it."[10]

Whether borne by one wife or two, Genesis attributes twelve sons and a daughter to Ishmael. The sons are presumed to have begun tribes of their own in Arabia, but the daughter, named Mahalath, moved to Canaan to become a daughter-in-law of Isaac and Rebekah when she married their son, Esau.

THE UNEXPECTED WIFE

Abraham was now "old, and well stricken in age." His sons were married, and grandchildren were beginning to arrive. His wife, Sarah, had died, as had His concubine, Hagar. It was a time to ease up a bit and bask in the sun. Or at least that would be the usual way of things if Abraham were a usual man. But He wasn't, so He opened a new chapter of His life on earth by marrying Keturah and fathering six sons with her.[11]

The name *Keturah*, which can also be spelled *Katurah, Cetura,* or *Qeturah*, has the meaning of *perfume* or *sweet-smelling incense*. Very little is known about her, except for a single suggestion that she was the daughter of two of Abraham's household servants, people who might originally have been from either Ur or Harran.[12]

Among the many questions people have about Keturah are whether she was a wife or a concubine, and whether she and Abraham were united while Sarah was still alive or after she died.

The New Testament mentions Keturah as a concubine, but the Old Testament and the Bahá'í writings agree in describing her as a wife. And although the sequence of Abraham's life as outlined in Genesis indicates that He and Keturah married after Sarah's death, that particular sequence may have more to do with the needs of laying out the story in an easy-to-follow form than with the actual order of events. It is quite possible that the union took place while Sarah was alive, but, even so, Keturah could still have been a true wife. As the Old Testament indicates time and time again, taking more than one wife—plus a cluster of concubines—was a common and accepted practice.

But, wife or concubine, the most significant bit of information about their union is that Keturah subsequently bore six sons, giving Abraham a grand total of eight male children. All of Abraham's seed would be blessed by God, and these six were indisputably part of the family. In order that the genealogy might be remembered and traced over the centuries, Genesis records it this way: "And she bare him Zimran, and Jokshan, and Medan, and Midian, and Ishbak, and Shuah." One of the six—Midian—receives the honor of having his children named: "Ephah, and Epher, and Hanoch, and Abidah, and Eldaah." Another—Jokshan—receives even more attention by having both children and grandchildren listed: "And Jokshan begat Sheba, and Dedan. And the sons of Dedan were Asshurim, and Letushim, and Leummim."[13]

After the six sons had been born, Abraham gave Keturah and the children gifts and, in the succinct but not-very-informative words of Genesis, sent them "eastward, unto to the east country."[14] Abraham was nearing the end of His life, and the destiny of this group of children lay not in Canaan but elsewhere. If, as suggested by the Book of Jubilees, Keturah's parents were originally from Ur of the Chaldees (which certainly can be described as *the east country*) she would have had tribal relatives there who would be happy to see her and delighted to meet her children.

The most common notion about what the sons did after leaving Canaan is that they and their descendants became involved in trading spices, silks, gems, and other goods. Midian moved northeast of Canaan—to the upper part of Arabia near the Gulf of Aqaba— and is credited with founding the Midianite tribe. Muḥammad mentions Midian several times in the Qur'án as *Madyan* and refers to the Midianite tribe as the *Madyan people.*

One of Midian's descendants, Jethro, makes an appearance in both Islam and Judaism. In the Qur'án, Jethro is called *Shu'aib* and is acclaimed as a prophet who was rejected by the other members of the Midianite / Madyan tribe. In Judaism, Jethro is chiefly remembered as having been the father-in-law of Moses, something that occurred when Moses fled to Midian from Egypt and married

Zipporah, who was one of Jethro's seven daughters. Zipporah was later instrumental in saving Moses' life, an incident that underlines the importance of Keturah's descendants.

Jokshan (the second son of Keturah and the father of Sheba and Dedan), is also thought to have settled in Arabia, somewhere along the western coast. This supposition is based primarily on the way that the names of his children correspond with Arabian geography. Sheba was a kingdom in southern Arabia, and Dedan (currently called "Al 'Ula") was an oasis along an ancient path that connected southwestern Arabia to Canaan and the Mediterranean. With the passing of centuries, the amount of traffic on the path increased (a single caravan might contain two thousand camels), and Dedan grew into a city. The path eventually became known as the "incense road" because the most prized products carried along it were aromatic nuggets of dried sap harvested from frankincense and myrrh trees growing in southern Arabia. The way that Keturah's name—*incense*—was applied to the route along which most of her sons settled is an intriguing congruence.

Zimran, too, is said to have settled in Arabia, but farther to the south than either Midian or Jokshan. His name has been linked with the town of Zabran, which once lay between Mecca and Medina.

Various cuneiform texts connect Shuah, the youngest son of Keturah and Abraham, with Syria. They place him in the land that was known as Sûchu or Suhi, an area that lies along the northern part of the Euphrates river.[15] The idea that Shuah succeeded in founding a tribe / kingdom bearing his name is reinforced by the book of Job in the Old Testament because several verses describe Job—who lived several hundred years after Shuah—as having a friend who was a Shuhite.

Shuah's slightly older brother, Ishbak, probably lived to the north of Shuah and founded a tribe of his own. Old Assyrian records affirm this by listing one of the northern Syrian tribes as "Iasbuq."[16*]

---

* Although I have suggested specific places where Keturah's sons settled, it is far more likely that the process by which they and their descendants moved to the east and became credited with being progenitors of tribes was a gradual one that extended over several generations.

The most mysterious of Keturah's sons is Medan, the third to be born. None of the sacred scriptures shed light on where he settled, but there have been suggestions that he lived southeast of Midian. There is also a very tenuous connection between his descendants (and / or the descendants of Midian) and the marsh dwellers of Mesopotamia—the same marsh that surrounded Ur when Abraham lived there—because the marsh dwellers are currently known as the *Medan* people (also *Ma'dān* or *Mi'dan*). Those who connect the marsh dwellers to Medan think that people from his tribe fled to the marshes and settled there to escape being killed during one of the many wars that swept across Syria and northern Iraq.*

Wherever Keturah's children really settled, the manner in which Abraham deliberately scattered six of his eight sons and their "gifts" along trade routes connecting three continents (Africa, Europe, and Asia) is charmingly symbolic. More than any other single event, the act of sharing so many sons with the larger world outside Canaan indicated that God's magnificent promise to Abraham really was meant to come true: "I will make your descendants as the dust of the earth; so that if a man can number the dust of the earth, then shall thy seed also be numbered."[17]

A FUNERAL

When Abraham did, at last, die, Ishmael and Isaac worked together to bury Him, though the exact timing of events is unclear. If Ishmael was already visiting because he had been summoned to the bedside of his ailing father, he and Isaac would have buried Abraham within a day or so of His death. Together—or with the help of servants—the brothers would have cleared out the shaft or tunnel leading to the Cave of Machpelah, which Abraham had so purposefully acquired. Once inside the small cave, they might have

---

* One objection to the idea that a son of Keturah—Medan and / or Midian—could have influenced the name of the marsh dwellers comes from a difference in meanings, though meanings often change over time. *Medan* or *Mi'dan*, as in marsh dweller, is usually translated as meaning *dwellers of the plain*. *Medan*, as in Keturah's son, means *judgment*, while *Midian* can mean either *strife* or *place of judgment*.

gathered the decomposed remnants of Sarah's body and placed the bones in a box or jar. Or they might have placed Abraham's corpse near where Sarah lay and left it to future generations to gather the bones of both parents and mingle them in a single container. A few treasured objects might have been placed in the tomb as well.

If Ishmael was summoned after Abraham's death, and if it took him days, weeks, or months to arrive, the burial of Abraham might have occurred in two stages. Within a day or so of death, His body would have been buried in a shallow pit, probably in a hillside cemetery area that the household had been using for years. The gravesite might have been marked with a rough tombstone or a terracotta jug half-buried in the earth. When Ishmael arrived, he and Isaac would have removed Abraham's desiccated remains, transferred them to a container, and placed the container in the Cave of Macphelah as Abraham intended.

As previously mentioned, the Cave of Machpelah in Hebron is thought to lie directly underneath a complex of buildings and shrines—some ancient, some newer—known as the Tomb of the Patriarchs. Because the shaft leading to the cave was hidden under the floor of the building erected to protect it, the exact location of the shaft was forgotten. It remained unknown for centuries until a monk, Arnulf, reportedly rediscovered it and entered the cave in AD 1119. Christian Crusaders were in control of the area at that time, and a group of them were reportedly so excited by Arnulf's discovery that they, too, entered the cave, gathered up the bones they found lying there, and carried them into the building above. The bones, it is said, were placed in reliquaries (decorated boxes) and buried beneath the floor of the central building of the Tomb of the Patriarchs rather than being returned to the cave. Then the shaft leading down to the double-chambered cave was resealed. Gruesomely, some of the bones were said to have been given or sold to important pilgrims before the reliquaries were buried.[18]

What today's visitors see when they enter the Tomb of the Patriarchs are several large, ornately-decorated cenotaphs (boxy structures approximately the size of a pickup truck) that aren't really tombs at all. They are nothing more than elaborate monuments built two thousand years ago, during the reign of Herod.[19] They are not thought to contain any bones, though no one has taken them apart to find out. If a few original bones do exist at the site, they are likely to be somewhere under the floor of the Tomb of the Patriarchs, still encased in the reliquaries buried by the Crusaders.

18

HINTING AT THE FUTURE

Now this is not the end.
It is not even the beginning of the end.
But it is, perhaps, the end of the beginning.
Winston Churchill[1]

The overture to a musical, such as *South Pacific* or *Phantom of the Opera*, contains bits and pieces of songs that are destined to be sung during the full performance. If you are sitting in a dark auditorium, listening to an overture for the very first time in your life, the music will be both tantalizing and mysterious. It will hint at events to come, yet from the overture alone, you will not be able to guess exactly what will happen. Only after the curtain rises and the actors have assumed their roles will the melodic snippets expand into songs and—one by one—reveal their full glory.

By stretching the musical analogy a bit, we can apply it to Abraham. Within the bounds of this analogy, Abraham's life was a tantalizing overture, full of prophetic hints about various songs that would be sung in the millennia ahead. When the overture ended—when Abraham died—it seemed to be the end of everything, but it was merely a necessary pause. Soon the curtain would rise on the full performance, and the prophetic overtones of His life would develop into complete melodies.

WELLS OF SPARKLING WATER

In addition to themes mentioned in previous chapters, a motif from Abraham's life that has been repeated in subsequent Revelations is that of the imagery of wells. Abraham was the first Messenger of God recorded as having dug a well. The wells He excavated to physically water His flocks of sheep simultaneously served as symbols of divine blessings and eternal life for His flock of believers. Abraham was also the first Messenger of God described as having had His wells filled in with rubble by neighboring tribes who did not want to drink from them. After Abraham died, Isaac dug the wells again and released fresh water, indicating that the spiritual processes set in motion by Abraham would not be permanently blocked.[2]

This scenario of releasing fresh water from wells has been repeated in all of the Abrahamic religions. Each Messenger has found that the "wells" of perception opened by previous Revelators have become filled with the "sludge" of misunderstanding, opposition, disobedience, and superstition. After removing the sludge, each of them has provided a fresh source of sparkling water for anyone willing to partake. Moses, for instance, gathered His congregation together near a dry rock and "with his rod he smote the rock twice: and the water came out abundantly, and the congregation drank, and their beasts also." Jesus offered "a well of water springing up into everlasting life." For Muḥammad, the symbolism of wells became quite literal when His grandfather presaged Muḥammad's Revelation by rediscovering the well of ZamZam, whose location had been lost, and clearing away the sand so water could again flow forth. The Báb described the water He was offering in mystical terms: "I give you to drink, by the leave of God, the sovereign Truth, of the crystal-pure waters of His Revelation which are gushing out from the incorruptible Fountain situate upon the Holy Mount." And Bahá'u'lláh enjoined those who seek knowledge to "Drink your fill from the wellspring of wisdom."[3]

MONOTHEISM

By smashing idols and speaking of a God Who was both invisible and indivisible, Abraham opened a new area of spiritual reality for humankind to investigate: monotheism. In spite of Abraham's foundation, however, when Moses began His ministry, He had to again explain and reinforce the idea of monotheism among people who were still thinking in very literal terms and retained a strong desire to worship solid idols. To get His point across, Moses used concrete idioms, describing God as a consuming fire Who was so jealous that He could be provoked to anger by anyone who dared carve an idol.[4]

More than a thousand years later, Jesus, speaking to people whose worldview was significantly different than that of the tribes who had lived during the time of Moses, was able to expand man's appreciation of the transcendence of God by portraying Him in ways that were less concrete and more ethereal. He spoke of God as a mystery and explained that "God is light, and in him is no darkness at all." Because Moses had already firmly implanted the concept of justice in Judaism, Jesus was able to spend more time emphasizing God's love, including the way in which it could be reflected by the human soul: "God is love; and he that dwelleth in love dwelleth in God, and God in him." And, as mentioned previously, Jesus also taught the world an incredible lesson about the nature of self-sacrifice.[5]

Muḥammad's challenge was that of spiritualizing a group of brutal desert tribes who "battled and pillaged mercilessly" and were willing to bury extra baby girls alive in the desert rather than bear the expense of feeding them. So although Muḥammad did speak of God as merciful, compassionate, and forgiving, He—like Moses—had to spend much of His time stressing the sterner aspects of the one Creator. "Whoso is an enemy to God," said Muḥammad, "shall have God as his enemy."[6]

Bahá'u'lláh, speaking nearly two thousand years after Jesus and fourteen hundred years after Muḥammad, validated all of the previous images by describing both fear and love as essential qualities of a faithful soul: "Their hearts are illumined with the light of the fear of God, and adorned with the adornment of His love." And then Bahá'u'lláh added one more perplexing layer to the conundrum that is God by emphasizing His complete transcendence: "To every discerning and illumined heart it is evident that God, the unknowable Essence, the divine Being, is immensely exalted beyond every human attribute, such as corporeal existence, ascent and descent, egress and regress. Far be it from His glory that human tongue should adequately recount His praise, or that human heart comprehend His fathomless mystery. He is and hath ever been veiled in the ancient eternity of His Essence, and will remain in His Reality everlastingly hidden from the sight of men."[7]

THE HOUSE OF GOD

Another theme from Abraham that has blossomed into a full aria is that of enclosing a sacred space where people can congregate to worship the invisible and indivisible God. According to Muhammad, "The first temple that was founded for mankind, was that in Becca"—the temple erected by Abraham and Ishmael. God commanded them to "Purify my house for those who shall go in procession round it, and those who shall abide there for devotion, and those who shall bow down and prostrate themselves [in prayer]."[8*]

Several special features made Abraham's temple different than any other religious structure of its time: It was not oriented toward the sky and stars above. It did not contain any idols, nor was it considered to be the dwelling place of a god. Furthermore, its use was not restricted to priests because anyone was allowed to enter it and pray.

---

* Later on, it became a Muslim tradition that Adam built the first temple and Abraham merely restored it, but this is not corroborated by any of the sacred scriptures.

By contrast, the enormous stone circles such as Stonehenge and the Ring of Brodgar, which seem to have served a religious purpose, were aimed at providing a view of the sky where divine portents might be observed at certain times of the year. And the jagged ziggurats of Mesopotamia were capped, it is thought, by small shrines at the top that were available to any god who was willing to come down from the sky and make it his home. The solid construction of the ziggurats—several platforms of sun-dried brick, each platform smaller than the one on which it rested—did not allow for the possibility of interior gatherings.

The religious structures of Egypt were not solid inside, like ziggurats, but the few rooms they did contain were not open to the general public. Instead, they served primarily as repositories for sacred objects and as homes for a god or a god's family. They were also places where priests conducted rites that were thought to provide protection to the pharaoh and his subjects. Ordinary citizens might be allowed into the courtyard of a temple to catch sight of an idol on a festival day, and a few lucky people might be allowed to enter an audience chamber to submit a question to one of the gods, but in general, use of the interior spaces was restricted to priests.[9]

The temple built by Abraham was a lopsided rectangle with the measurement of each of the four sides being somewhere between thirty and forty-nine feet. Abraham placed a football-sized rock, which geologists suggest may be an agate, somewhere inside the room, maybe in a niche in the easternmost wall.[10] The stone fractured into several pieces during a fire following a battle in AD 683, but it was later reassembled, set within a metal frame, and embedded in one of the walls, where it can still be seen. The purpose of the stone isn't known, but it could have been a transitional object—a means of helping worshippers abandon idols by giving them a marked direction toward which they could bow or kneel in prayer.

Abraham's temple, originally known simply as *House of God,* has been refurbished and rebuilt several times, making it impossible to know whether the original structure was of wood or stone, though it is reasonable to suppose that it was constructed of local granite with a wood roof supported by several pillars. A series of renovations during the following centuries changed the sizes of the walls and pushed the ceiling higher, making the structure more like a cube. The name by which the building is currently known—*Kaaba* or *Ka'bah* or *Caaba*—refers to the Arabic word for *cube* and was applied to the building only after the all the changes in its appearance had been finished.

No matter its name, the Kaaba served several important purposes in the centuries after Abraham's death. It was a place where God could be worshipped by ordinary people as well as a venue for community gatherings, such as the poetry contests that were popular among the Arabian tribes. The House of God was considered such sacred, neutral territory that even the most bitter of adversaries would suspend their disagreements while in its vicinity, a practice that made Mecca a relatively peaceful city and allowed it to prosper as a center of trade. Now and then, a person fleeing for his life from an enemy would take refuge inside the House of God because no one was allowed to enter it for the purpose of revenge or violence.[11]

As the renown of the Kaaba spread, pilgrims came to it from places outside of Arabia, including Jews from Canaan. It was even mentioned in an ancient travel guide by Diodorus Siculus, a Greek historian of the first century BC. In his book *Bibliotheca Historica*, the section on Arabia included these words about Mecca: "'And a temple has been set up there, which is very holy and exceedingly revered by all Arabians.'"[12]

Following the pattern set by Abraham, synagogues, churches, mosques, and Bahá'í temples are alike in that they are dedicated to the worship of an invisible / indivisible God who does not live inside a specific idol or shrine. The structures are not oriented toward a particular view of the stars, nor is their use limited to a special class of clergy. They are not meant to be admired only from the outside but derive their true purpose from the way they invite believers to come inside and worship together. And, like the original

House of God, these sacred spaces have often become important centers of community life because they have hosted functions other than that of worship, such as classes for children, weddings, concerts, and even town meetings.

A SUCCESSION OF MESSENGERS

One of the most mysterious but all-embracing themes sounded within the story of Abraham's life as laid out in the book of Genesis is that of anticipation of the future. Hints about the roles that will be played by various descendants of Abraham are woven into the story as generously and beautifully as sequins on a tutu. The next several chapters will consider some of the ways in which those glittering hints have been fulfilled by five Messengers of God and will outline their genealogies as well.

19

MOSES

. . . the Sun of reality
poured forth its rays from the sign of Abraham,
and then it dawned from the sign of Moses
and illuminated the horizon.
'Abdu'l-Bahá[1]

When Isaac was born to Sarah, he was given the first right of inheritance over his older half-brother Ishmael. This act can be construed as a hint that the first line of descent to bear fruit, the first to produce Messengers of God after Abraham, would be from Sarah rather than from Hagar or Keturah. Moses, born a few hundred years after Abraham, was that Messenger.

Moses was born in Egypt to Amram and his wife, Jochebed, who were both Levites, a tribe deriving its name from a great-grandson of Abraham and Sarah named Levi. The Levites were living in Egypt because famine had driven Levi's father, Jacob, out of Canaan. During their stay in Egypt, Jacob's family and the other Hebrews who had emigrated from Canaan had prospered, so they opted to remain there. After several generations, the former Canaanites hardly thought of themselves as anything except Egyptian, though they were still considered outsiders by the rest of the populace. And though they did manage to remember the God of Abraham, they soon became accustomed to worshipping some of the same idols that the Egyptians held dear and, in the process, forgot many of Abraham's teachings.

Moses was born at a time when, according to the book of Exodus, a new pharaoh had come to power who did not appreciate the way in which the Hebrews had prospered and multiplied. Thinking to limit their numbers, he enacted a harsh law: Egyptians were ordered to fling any son who was born to a Hebrew into the Nile, but the daughters were to be spared. With this kind of population control, no young Hebrew males would be available for the daughters to marry when they matured. The young women would then marry Egyptians and be assimilated into Egyptian society. By the end of a full generation, the Hebrews would cease to be a separate race or ethnic group.

Looking for a hint of prophetic fulfillment in this harsh pharaonic edict, one can see that the words Abraham spoke to Sarah when they entered Egypt might well have foretold what would someday happen to these beleaguered male and female descendants: "they will kill me (a male) while you (a female) they will let live."[2]

Moses' mother, Jochebed, managed to hide Moses from the eye of every searching Egyptian for three months. Then, knowing she "could no longer hide him, she took a wicker ark for him and caulked it with resin and pitch and placed the child in it and placed it in the reeds by the banks of the Nile."[3]

Because she desperately wanted to know what would happen to her son—and, conceivably, because she had a plan—Jochebed asked Moses' older sister to keep watch.

As the sister watched, she saw a princess accompanied by her serving girls walk down to the edge of the river to bathe. When the princess spied the basket-ark bobbing among the reeds, she told one of the servants to fetch it. The princess took the basket, opened it, and found the baby boy inside. She realized right away that He was one of the Hebrew children, but His helpless cries touched her heart, and she did not fling the baby into the river.

Observing that the princess did not immediately obey the law of her father (the pharaoh), Moses' sister boldly approached and asked, "Shall I go and summon a nursing woman from the Hebrews that she may suckle the child for you?"[4]

The princess must not have liked her father's genocidal plan because she agreed to the little girl's offer. Moses' sister fetched their mother, Jochebed, and the princess—without realizing Jochebed was the true mother—hired her to nurse the baby until he was old enough to be adopted into the royal household.

After the adoption had taken place, the princess said she would call Him Moses, a name that has meaning in both Hebrew and Egyptian. In Hebrew, it sounds similar to the term *mosheh—drawn out*—and refers to the way the baby was taken out of the water. In Egyptian, *mos* means *child* or *one who is born*, and it was often used as part of a pharaoh's name. *Thutmose*, for example, means *one who was born of the god Thoth* or *child of Thoth*. So by using the name without attaching it to a particular god, perhaps the princess was slyly indicating that Moses was born, seemingly, out of thin air.

The story of Moses floating to safety in a teeny-tiny ark can be seen as a reenactment of something experienced by a previous Messenger of God—Noah. In the same way that Noah's ark (whether a literal or a mystical ark or both) saved a remnant of humankind, this baby's ark carried Him to safety so He would be able to grow up and "save" those who became His followers.[5]

Even though Moses grew up thinking of Himself as a high-ranking Egyptian, He was aware of His background. As He grew older, He spent time watching what was happening to His relatives, many of whom had, under the current pharaoh, been forced into a position of virtual slavery and were doing hard labor under brutal overseers. When, one fine day, He saw an Egyptian unfairly beating a worker, he looked around to see who would help stop this injustice. No help appeared, and the beating continued. Moses, finding the scene unbearable, intervened; He killed the Egyptian man and buried him in the sand.

The next day, Moses came across a second scene of violence, but this time it was two Hebrews who were fighting each other. He attempted to remonstrate with them, saying to the offender, "Why are you hitting your fellow Hebrew?" The offender was not all abashed. Belligerently, he retorted, "Who made you ruler and judge over us? Are you thinking of killing me as you killed the Egyptian?"[6] Hearing these words, Moses realized that the killing had become known, and He must also have realized that His own kin resented Him enough to believe He had no right to impose any form of justice on them.

When the pharaoh heard about the killing, he ordered the execution of Moses, but Moses left Egypt and fled to the land of Midian, where "he sat down by a well."[7] Midian, of course, is the land settled by one of the sons of Abraham's third wife, Keturah, and it would seem that the mention of a well is a reminder that Moses was destined to drink from one of the wells of spiritual understanding that had first been opened by Abraham.

Moses married and remained in Midian for several years. While He was there, He reflected on what had happened in Egypt, and "He asked God—exalted be His glory—to forgive Him, and He was forgiven."[8]

The realization of the nature of His spiritual mission came to Moses while He was tending a herd of goats in the wilderness. He described the experience as hearing an angel speak from the midst of a bush that burned without being consumed, which recalls the way Abraham was able to stand firm and speak the truth from within the fire of polytheism. When Moses approached the bush, God began to speak, instructing Him to talk to the pharaoh and deliver the Hebrews from their bondage, presumably from the spiritual bondage of being loyal to something other than the legacy of Abraham as well as the physical bondage they were currently enduring in Egypt.

God further instructed Moses to say, "The Lord God of your fathers, the God of Abraham, the God of Isaac, and the God of Jacob, sent me to you." And so it was that Moses' difficult life as a

Messenger of God to the Hebrews—who were also known as the sons of Israel, or Israelites, but not yet as Jews—began.[9]*

The life of Moses held a number of reminders that all three of Abraham's wives—and their descendants—were an important part of God's plan for humanity. First of all, Moses was descended from Sarah. Like her, He was taken in but subsequently ejected by a pharaoh. Second, Moses was born in Hagar's homeland of Egypt, yet had to leave it—as she did—and settle in Canaan. There is also a nice coincidence between the tradition that Hagar was the daughter of a pharaoh and the fact that Moses was raised by a daughter of a pharaoh. And, third, when Moses traveled to the land of Midian, seeking wisdom from one of its wells, He took a descendant of Keturah—Zipporah—as His first wife.

Moses' achievements were remembered and celebrated by the Abrahamic Messengers who followed Him. Jesus reminded people of the magnificent way in which God had spoken to Moses. Muḥammad told His followers that God "gave the Scripture unto Moses, complete for him who would do good, an explanation of all things, a guidance and a mercy, that they might believe in the meeting with their Lord." Bahá'u'lláh recounted the glory of Moses by saying, "Armed with the rod of celestial dominion, adorned with the white hand of divine knowledge, and proceeding from the Párán of the love of God, and wielding the serpent of power and everlasting majesty, He shone forth from the Sinai of light upon the world."[10]

---

* The term *Jews* was, at first, a designation used only for members of the tribe of Judah, which claimed its descent from Levi's brother, Judah. Centuries later, after war and deportation had affected the balance of Israelite tribes and left those from Judah in the majority, the terms *Jew* and *Judaism* began to be used to refer to the religion and to all those of Hebrew descent.

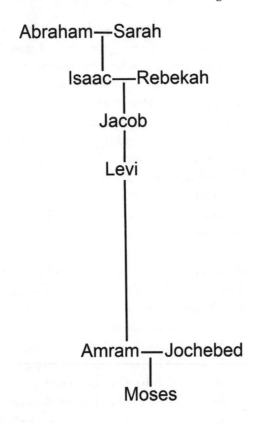

Simplified genealogy of Moses

20

JESUS THE CHRIST

*Moses gave the message of the glad tidings of Christ,
and Christ confirmed the Prophethood of Moses.
Therefore, between Moses and Jesus
there is no variation or conflict.*
'Abdu'l-Bahá[1]

More than a thousand years after Moses, the second Messenger of God to rise from Abraham and Sarah's line was Jesus. During His ministry, Jesus drew a line from the past to the present, making it clear that the God with which He communed was the same God Who had appeared to Abraham and spoken to Moses. "Have ye not read in the book of Moses," Jesus asked, "in the account of the bush, how God said to him 'I am the God of Abraham, and the God of Isaac, and the God of Jacob?'" Furthermore, Jesus reminded His listeners that the past and the present were connected to the future because God had made promises "to Abraham and his descendants forever."[2]

Jesus reaffirmed the importance of the Ten Commandments that Moses had brought and then, in His capacity as a Manifestation of God, gave several new laws, including a very stringent edict about divorce and a heartwarming decree concerning love: "A new command I give unto you. Love one another. As I have loved you, so you must love one another."[3]

It was difficult for many of those who heard Jesus' message to believe that He was truly a Messiah because the manner in which He fulfilled the prophecies of the Old Testament did not jibe with people's completely literal expectations. They were looking forward to someone who would be born in a city they'd never heard of, a warrior-king who would sit on an imposing throne and conquer East and West with a flick of his iron sword. Furthermore, the new prophet would be an animal-tamer of astounding ability because he would convince wolves to lie down peacefully among lambs.

To the consternation of most of those who met Him, Jesus' life did not match their expectations. He was born in a city everyone had heard of. He was too humble to claim a throne and be crowned as a king and too peaceful to own a sword or command an army. Speaking in Paris in 1911, 'Abdu'l-Bahá described the spiritual paradoxes posed by the advent of Jesus in these terms:

> Although He came from Nazareth, which was a known place, He also came from Heaven. His body was born of Mary, but His Spirit came from Heaven. The sword He carried was the sword of His tongue, with which He divided the good from the evil, the true from the false, the faithful from the unfaithful, and the light from the darkness. His Word was indeed a sharp sword! The Throne upon which He sat is the Eternal Throne from which Christ reigns forever, a heavenly throne, not an earthly one, for the things of earth pass away but heavenly things pass not away. He reinterpreted and completed the Law of Moses and fulfilled the Law of the Prophets. His word conquered the East and the West. His Kingdom is everlasting . . . The animals who were to live with one another signified the different sects and races, who, once having been at war, were now to dwell in love and charity, drinking together the water of life from Christ the Eternal Spring.[4]

AN ANCESTRAL RIDDLE

Another puzzling facet of Jesus' life is the matter of His genetic lineage. In retelling the story of Jesus, two of the Gospels of the New Testament—Matthew and Luke—provide detailed genealogies, but their long lists raise as many questions as they answer.

Matthew is thought to have been one of the Twelve Apostles, though it is difficult to be certain that the apostle named Matthew is identical with the Gospel writer. In any case, the Gospel of Matthew traces Jesus' ancestors back through forty generations to Abraham. Luke, by contrast, was a Greek physician who never met Jesus. His writings reflect a love of historical details, and his genealogy is much more extensive than that of Matthew. Luke traces four thousand years of ancestry by following the trail beyond Abraham and going all the way back to "Adam, which was the son of God."[5]

Among the multitude of fascinating puzzles presented by the two genealogies are a couple of especially riveting items: First, neither genealogy traces Jesus' biological inheritance. Both Matthew and Luke are quite clear in stating that they are tracing the lineage of Joseph, who was Jesus' adopted father but not His biological father.

Second, the two genealogies don't fully agree. Matthew and Luke each trace Joseph back to Abraham through King David, who lived c. 1000 BC, but they take different routes to get there. Matthew begins by naming the father of Joseph as Jacob, while Luke names the man who was probably Jacob's brother or half-brother—Eli (or Heli)—as Joseph's father.

There have been numerous explanations of why the genealogies differ. Many of them are focused on proving that one of the genealogies is Mary's, which would make King David a genetic ancestor of Jesus. King David is cherished in both Judaism and Christianity because several Old Testament prophets foresaw that David's house would be eternally important, that a ruler from David's family would restore Israel and usher in an era of peace, and that God would "establish the throne of [David's] kingdom forever."[6] Those who believe that Jesus was the Messenger intended to fill these promises genetically rather than spiritually are eager to connect Him to David.

But, tempting as it may be to assign Jesus to the line of David (within the tribe of Judah), many scholarly sources, including the Catholic Encyclopedia, conclude that there is no valid way of claiming that either of the genealogies in the New Testament belongs to Mary. The Encyclopedia suggests, instead, that Jesus be connected to David through adoption: "If by virtue of Joseph's marriage with Mary, Jesus could be called the son of Joseph, he can for the same reason be called 'son of David.'"[7]

Digging even deeper into the question of descent, one discovers in the New Testament that Mary is a cousin of Elizabeth, who is a Levite through Aaron, who was the brother of Moses and, like Him, a son of Amram. This makes Elizabeth—and by extension, Mary—a descendant of Abraham through Sarah but not through David. This lineage is explained more clearly in the Qur'án when Muḥammad describes Mary's mother as being "a woman of 'Imran," which means she was definitely a descendant of Moses' father, Amram. The Bahá'í writings concur by explicitly placing Joseph rather than Mary in the line of David.[8]

DISMISSING GENEALOGY

When Jesus Himself was asked about His ancestors, He dismissed the question of lineage entirely, replying, "My kingdom is not of this world." Or, as the Bahá'í writings describe it, "In reality His Holiness Christ was glorified with an eternal sovereignty and everlasting dominion, spiritual and not temporal. His throne and kingdom were established in human hearts where He reigns with power and authority without end."[9]

Throughout His short ministry, sitting upon a spiritual throne in a nonphysical kingdom, Jesus invited everyone, Jew or gentile, circumcised or uncircumcised, woman or man, poor or rich, to follow Him. And through this persistent focus on faith rather than family background, a wonderful thing happened. Jesus inaugurated a new era of accepting a religion by choice rather than by DNA.

This fresh and exciting understanding of the role of religion allowed monotheism to escape its tribal confinement in the Middle East and spread to diverse cultures and other continents, eventually becoming the most widespread religion on earth. Thus God's promise to make Abraham's seed a blessing to the whole world was fulfilled through Jesus the Christ in a mystical manner that no one had anticipated and that no one could really understand until centuries later.

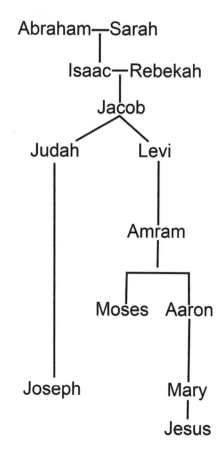

Simplified genealogy of Jesus

21

MUḤAMMAD

We believe in God,
and what has been revealed to us,
and what has been revealed to
Abraham, and Ishmael, and Isaac, and Jacob, and the Tribes,
and what was brought to Moses and Jesus,
and what was brought unto the Prophets from their Lord;
we will not distinguish between any one of them,
and unto Him are we resigned.
Muḥammad[1]

In AD 582 or thereabouts, an Arabian trading caravan led by a man named Abu Talib was making its way north from Mecca to Damascus. To escape the overbearing heat of the midday, it stopped to rest just inside the southern border of Syria, near the town of Bosra. The riders dismounted and tethered their camels within sight of a Christian monastery that had been occupied for years by solitary monks. When the current monk died, another would come to take his place. Each monk had students who came to learn from him, and there were servants on the premises, so the monastery had a number of rooms in it, including a library filled with manuscripts.

The monk of AD 582 was known as Bahira. He loved the monastery's library and had immersed himself in the study of its manuscripts, which probably included several versions of the Old and the New Testaments. Reading through the manuscripts, he would have become familiar with the verses concerning Ishmael and the promises made to Hagar that a great nation would be created though her descendants. Living not far from Mecca, he must also have been regaled by local accounts of how Abraham and Ishmael had built the Kaaba, and, if so, he could have linked that event with the verse in Psalms (84:6) that speaks of Baca (Mecca).[2]

In his musings, Bahira might have wondered about the implications of God's promise to Moses that because the Israelites had begged at Mt. Sinai to never again be forced to hear the voice of God themselves, He would raise up a Prophet who would be like Moses but who would come from the brethren of the Israelites (i.e. from the half-brothers of Isaac). After reading these prophecies in the Book of Deuteronomy, Bahira might have connected them with the words in the Book of Isaiah describing a servant from the lineage of Kedar (a son of Ishmael) who would someday bring justice, prevail against His enemies and cause people to sing a *new song* (i.e., follow a new religion).[3]

Like many other Christians of his time, Bahira would have been curious about the promise made by Jesus that after His crucifixion, God would send *another* Counselor. This new Counselor would, like Jesus, be a flesh-and-blood person who nevertheless possessed the authority of the Holy Spirit. This next Counselor would also bear witness to the truth of what Jesus had said, and various translations of the New Testament refer to this event as the coming of the Paraclete, the Comforter, the Helper, the Counselor, or the Advocate:

> And I will ask the Father, and he will give you another Counselor to be with you forever.[4]

> When the Helper comes, whom I will send to you from the Father—even the Spirit of true knowledge who comes from the Father—he will give witness about me.[5]

Nevertheless I tell you the truth; It is expedient for you that
I go away: for if I go not away, the Comforter will not come
unto you; but if I depart, I will send him unto you.[6]

But the Paraclete, the Holy Ghost, whom the Father will send
in my name, he will teach you all things, and bring all things
to your mind, whatsoever I shall have said to you.[7]

As the caravan of Abu Talib neared the monastery, Bahira
watched the string of camels moving slowly toward him and noticed something odd. A cloud or shadow seemed to hover above one
of the camels. Fascinated, Bahira continued to watch and wonder.
When the caravan stopped to rest, the cloud also stopped and began hovering directly above one of the trees at the oasis, providing
extra shade to the people sitting below. It even seemed to Bahira
that the branches of the tree managed to lower themselves in order
to deepen the shade.

Realizing that the vision he had experienced must have been
caused by the spiritual potency of one of the members of the caravan, Bahira rushed out of monastery. He approached the traders,
greeted their leader, and invited everyone to join him for a meal.

When the men from the caravan entered, Bahira scrutinized
each face but did not find what he expected to see. Puzzled, he
asked if everyone had come inside. "There is not one that hath
been left behind," they answered, "save only a boy, the youngest
of us all."

At Bahira's insistence, the boy was invited inside. His name
was Muḥammad, His face was radiant, and, with a single glance,
Bahira decided He must have caused the vision of the shadow-
ing cloud. To confirm his guess, Bahira asked Muḥammad several
questions about His life. Then he questioned Abu Talib, who was
Muḥammad's uncle, about their ancestors. After listening to the
answers, Bahira spoke gravely to Abu Talib: "Take thy brother's son
back to his country, and guard him . . . Great things are in store for
this brother's son of thine."[8]

THE FAMILY TREE

Muḥammad, like Jesus, did not claim to be a Prophet by virtue of His ancestry but by virtue of being appointed by God. His genealogy is, nevertheless, of great interest.

According to biblical testimony, Ishmael had twelve sons, each of whom founded a tribe. All of them settled between Egypt and Assyria—a location that would correspond to northern Egypt. Muslim tradition agrees with this assessment, and the residents of northern Arabia have long acknowledged their descent from Ishmael. Muḥammad was born to one of the tribes linked to that descent—the Quraysh—and the Quraysh believed their specific link to Ishmael came through his second son, Kedar, the same son who was named in the Book of Isaiah.

When Bahira questioned Abu Talib about his nephew's ancestry, this vital piece of information must have been exactly what he was hoping to hear. And thus it was that a scholarly monk who was well versed in the sacred scriptures of the first two Abrahamic religions became one of the first people to recognize the spiritual power of the boy Who would grow up to be the Founder of the third Abrahamic religion: Islam.

Because there is no unbroken chain of birth certificates, formal genealogies composed by Muslim historians for Muḥammad contain many of the same kinds of question marks that the genealogies of Jesus do. Even so, the assertion of a connection between Ishmael and Muḥammad possesses great historical and religious legitimacy, and its reality is recognized by the Bahá'í writings.[9]

HONORING OTHER RELIGIONS

During Muḥammad's life, He spoke often of Abraham and praised Him as the Founder of monotheism: "Say: God speaketh truth. Follow, therefore, the religion of Abraham, the sound in faith, who was not one of those who joined other gods to God."[10]

Besides speaking of Abraham, Muḥammad testified to the validity of Judaism and Christianity, saying, for example, "We gave Moses the Book and we followed him up with other apostles, and we gave Jesus the son of Mary manifest signs and aided him with the Holy Spirit." He also pointed out, somewhat humorously, that those who enjoy arguing over whether Abraham was essentially Jewish or truly Christian are missing the point: "O people of the Book, why do ye dispute about Abraham, when the law and the gospel were not revealed until after him?"[11]

Although Muhammad often chided Jews and Christians for not being fully obedient to the teachings of Moses and Jesus, He was careful to honor them as "People of the Book," and He did something new in the world of religion by outlining specific protections for them in the Qur'án. He also recognized the legitimacy of other religions by explaining that religious diversity was created by God for the specific purpose of testing whether or not each person is being true to the faith he or she professes: "To each of you God has prescribed a Law and a Way. If God would have willed, He would have made you a single people. But God's purpose is to test you in which he has given each of you, so strive in the pursuit of virtue, and know that you will all return to God [in the Hereafter], and He will resolve all the matters in which you disagree."[12]

Muhammad stated quite clearly that religious choice should be left up to the individual and not brought about by force, saying, "Let there be no compulsion in religion." Furthermore, He illuminated this injunction with very detailed—and peaceful—instructions about how to teach this new faith to others: "Say to those who have received the Book, and to the common folk, Do ye surrender yourselves unto God? If they become Muslims, then are they guided aright: but if they turn away—thy duty is only preaching; and God's eye is on His servants."[13]

Muhammad's success in fostering amicable relationships among the Abrahamic religions was nicely demonstrated by an unusual gathering that took place a few years before He died. Islamic scholar Karen Armstrong describes it this way: ". . . a delegation of sixty Christians with scholars and judges among them arrived in Medina from the southern capitol of Najran. In a kind of interfaith council rare in those days, Muslims and Christians, joined by Medina's Jewish rabbis, sat together discussing and arguing the meaning of their beliefs. This occurred at a time when, not far to the north, Christians and Persians had been engaged for decades in massively destructive religious wars. According to Muslim chroniclers, when the council in Medina ended, the Najran Christians mounted their camels and rode peacefully back home."[14]

TWELVE PRINCES

Another significant connection between Muḥammad and Ishmael is the promise God made to Abraham: "Behold, I have blessed him, and will make him fruitful, and will multiply him exceedingly; twelve princes shall he beget, and I will make him a great nation."[15] Although some biblical scholars try to connect the twelve princes with the twelve sons of Ishmael who founded tribes, a different interpretation is found in Shia Islam, and it connects directly to the Abrahamic religion that followed Islam: the Bábí Faith.

Before Muḥammad died, He indicated that 'Alí, a man who was His cousin as well as His son-in-law, was the one to whom Muslims should turn for guidance. He did not, however, put this in writing. After Muḥammad's death, many of His followers, especially those from tribes that had been rivals of the tribe of Muḥammad's father, decided to choose a leader rather than follow the guidance of 'Alí. They therefore elected a man named Abu Bakr and gave him the title of *caliph.*

The appointment of Abu Bakr had the effect of splitting Islam into two big groups: the Sunni, who were content with the new caliph, and the Shia, who believed 'Alí had been appointed by Muḥammad and was the true spiritual leader. The split was temporarily mended when 'Alí was named as the fourth caliph, but after he was assassinated and his son was forced out of office, the split deepened.

After the death of 'Alí, Sunni Muslims continued to be governed by a series of caliphs who were not necessarily related to Muḥammad genealogically. Shia Muslims, who were in the minority, had to obey the caliphs in political matters, but they continued to turn to 'Alí's successors for spiritual guidance. The Shia referred to 'Alí and his successors as *imams*. Each imam was a descendant of Muḥammad, and this chain of spiritual leaders continued for twelve generations. At that point, the son of the eleventh imam, who was still very young when he inherited the position of being the twelfth imam from his father, mysteriously disappeared.

According to the Shia understanding of what had happened, these twelve imams were the "twelve princes" promised to Hagar and Ishmael. Because the twelfth disappeared under mysterious circumstances, and his body was never recovered, Shia scholars began connecting him to certain prophecies in Islam, some of which had been given by previous imams. These prophecies talked about the coming of a promised redeemer of Islam who would restore justice and establish a new religion with different laws and a new Book. Appearing as a messianic figure called the *Mahdi* or the *Qá'im*, this redeemer would accompany the return of Jesus during the "Day of Resurrection" just as John the Baptist had accompanied His first appearance. [16]

Sunni Islam ignored the idea of a return of the twelfth imam, but it agreed with the coming of a redeemer who would, alongside Jesus, rid the world of error, injustice, and tyranny. And both sects identified the redeemer / Mahdi / Qá'im as a descendant of Muḥammad, which meant He would also be a descendant, ultimately, of Abraham and Hagar.[17]

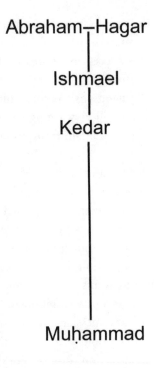

Simplified genealogy of Muḥammad

22

THE BÁB

We, verily, believe in Him Who,
in the person of the Báb,
hath been sent down by the Will of the one true God,
the King of Kings, the All-Praised.
Bahá'u'lláh[1]

On May 23, 1844, in Shiraz, Persia (Iran), a young man, just twenty-four years old, announced that He was the bearer of a long-promised divine Revelation destined to transform the spiritual life of the human race. The very next day, on the other side of the earth, Samuel F. B. Morse sent the first telegraph message in history. The message, which originated in Washington, D.C., and was received in Baltimore, said, "What hath God wrought."[2]

For both Christians and Muslims, it was an exciting time. Many Christian sects expected (on the basis of mathematical calculations from the Book of Daniel) that Jesus was due to return any minute. Some Christians camped on hillsides to await Him. Others, notably the German Templars, sold their possessions, left their homes, and moved to the foot of Mt. Carmel in Haifa, Israel, because they believed it would be the site of His appearance. In Islam, and especially in Shia Islam, several spiritual leaders thought that the time of the appearance of the Qá'im or Mahdi was near.

To Christians, who did not see Jesus descend from clouds in the sky, it seemed that their millennial expectations must have been mistaken (although Bahá'ís would say that they were spiritually correct). In the world of Islam, however, the announcement by a young man that He was the promised Qá'im produced an enormous shock wave. Those who accepted His Message did so because they believed that He was the Mahdi, the return of the twelfth imam, the promised redeemer of Islam.

The name of the young man was 'Alí-Muḥammad, but He took the mystical title of *Báb*, which means *Gate* or *Door*. His mission was unique in religious history because He was both a herald (like John the Baptist) and a Manifestation (like Jesus or Moses), and He brought a distinctly different Revelation with new sacred writings and several new laws.[3] The Báb founded a new religion—the Bábí Faith—whose primary purpose was, He explained, to open a portal of spiritual understanding through which an even greater Messenger would soon come. This new Messenger would usher in the age of peace and justice promised by previous Abrahamic faiths and other world religions as well.

The events surrounding the Declaration of the Báb and its effect on Islam were so profound that they were reported in the newspapers and magazines of other countries. One of the first articles appeared in the London Times in 1845. Under the title "Mahometan Schism," it reported the arrest of four of the Báb's earliest followers, who were punished for abandoning Islam. The authorities set the beards of the Bábís on fire, laced string through their noses, and yanked on the string to force them to march through the streets.[4]

The number of followers of the Báb increased rapidly, but so did the level of opposition by the clergy and by the ruler of Persia, Náṣiri'd-Dín S̲h̲áh. Within the span of six short years, hundreds of Bábis were tortured and / or killed. The writings of the Báb were condemned through a fatwa issued jointly by several religious scholars, and the Báb Himself was put to death by a firing squad in 1850.[5]

The Báb traced His ancestry to Muḥammad through Muḥammad's grandson, Ḥusayn, who was the third Imam of Shia Islam. This was the same Ḥusayn who sacrificed his life in an attempt to turn Islam from following what he thought was an incorrect and overly violent interpretation of Muḥammad's teachings (see chapter 15). Thus the Báb was a descendant of Muḥammad and, farther back, a descendant of Abraham and Hagar.

Just as each previous Messenger of God mentioned the Revelators who had preceded Him, the Báb referred to His spiritual predecessors, too. He explained their common purpose as that of reflecting God's word to man: "In the time of the First Manifestation the Primal Will appeared in Adam; in the day of Noah It became known in Noah; in the day of Abraham in Him; and so in the day of Moses; the day of Jesus; the day of Muḥammad, the Apostle of God . . ."[6]

The Báb delineated His position as being the current link in a coherent and continuous chain of Revelations. Believing in Him was synonymous with believing in the Messengers of the past: "He Who is the Eternal Truth beareth me witness, whoso followeth this Book [i.e., the Báb's Revelation] hath indeed followed all the past scriptures which have been sent down from heaven by God, the Sovereign Truth."[7]

One of the many sad events of the Báb's life was the death of His only child, a son, shortly after his birth. According to the journalistic narrative written by Nabíl-i-Aʻzam, a follower of the Báb, the baby's death was understood by the Báb as being a sacrifice akin to the one Abraham had been willing to make. Although he did not provide an exact quotation, Nabíl reported the way the Báb spoke of it in these words:

O God, my God! Would that a thousand Ishmaels were given Me, this Abraham of Thine, that I might have offered them, each and all, as a loving sacrifice unto Thee . . . O my God, my only Desire! Grant that the sacrifice of My son, My only son, may be acceptable unto Thee. Grant that it be a prelude to the sacrifice of My own, My entire self, in the path of Thy good pleasure. Endue with Thy grace My life-blood which I yearn to shed in Thy path. Cause it to water and nourish the seed of Thy Faith. Endow it with Thy celestial potency, that this infant seed of God may soon germinate in the hearts of men, that it may thrive and prosper, that it may grow to become a mighty tree, beneath the shadow of which all the peoples and kindreds of the earth may gather . . .[8]

After the Báb had been executed by a firing squad in 1850, the remains of His body were surreptitiously gathered by some of His followers and hidden. The box containing the remains was taken from Shiraz to Tehran, where it remained for almost fifty years. In the meantime, most of those who had been Bábís recognized Bahá'u'lláh as the Messenger promised by the Báb, and they became Bahá'ís. These converts regarded the extraordinary appearance of two Messengers of God within the same century as a fulfillment of Qur'ánic verses describing the sounding of two trumpet blasts that would shake the earth and cause men's hearts to quake.[9]

In 1899, the box containing the remains of the Báb was laboriously moved from Tehran to Palestine / Israel by Bahá'ís who carried it overland to Beirut and then by sea to Acre. A few years later, the remains of the Báb were entombed in a stone mausoleum built on the side of Mt. Carmel in Haifa. Following that, a shrine was erected atop the mausoleum, and in 2008, the Shrine of the Báb was designated as a World Heritage Site.

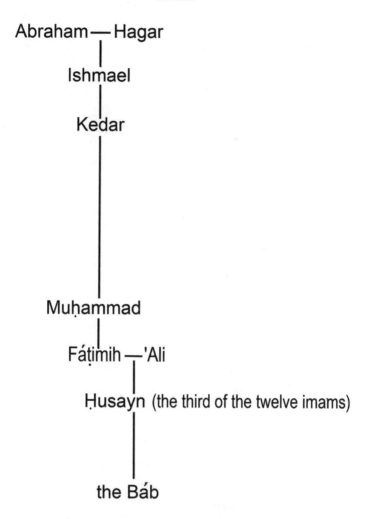

Simplified genealogy of the Báb

23

BAHÁ'U'LLÁH

I testify, O my God,
that if I were given a thousand lives by Thee,
and offered them up all in Thy path,
I would still have failed to repay
the least of the gifts which, by Thy grace,
Thou hast bestowed upon me.
Bahá'u'lláh[1]

Born in 1817, Bahá'u'lláh was two years older than the Báb. His father was an advisor to the shah, and the family was quite wealthy, owning houses in both Tehran and Mázindarán. When Bahá'u'lláh was just twenty-two years old, His father died. Bahá'u'lláh became head of the large household (His father had four wives, three concubines, and seventeen children, several of whom were still young). Everyone expected Him to assume His father's position in the shah's court, but He refused to follow a political path. Instead, He spent a great deal of time using His inherited wealth to minister to the needs of the less fortunate, and within a few years, He acquired the nickname *Father of the Poor*. Bahá'u'lláh's wife, Navváb, who wholeheartedly assisted Him, was affectionately referred to as the *Mother of Consolation*.

Less than three months after the Báb announced His Mission, Bahá'u'lláh learned of it. And even though this new religion, the Bábí Faith, was regarded by the powers of the day as a threat to the existing political and ecclesiastical order, Bahá'u'lláh declared Himself a follower and began teaching others about it. In 1848, He was arrested for this activity and punished by being bastinadoed (having the soles of his feet beaten until they bled).

After the Báb was executed by a firing squad in 1850, there was a concerted effort to obliterate the Bábí Faith. More than a thousand Bábís were killed, and many were tortured. Numerous others were arrested, including Bahá'u'lláh. For four months, He was imprisoned in a filthy underground prison in Tehran, where He was forced to wear a hundred-pound chain around His neck while His feet were immobilized by stocks.

During His short ministry, the Báb, like John the Baptist, had warned those who would listen that a Messenger greater than He would soon appear. During His imprisonment, Bahá'u'lláh was summoned to His destiny as that very Messenger, an experience He later described in these terms: "I lay asleep on the bed of self when lo, Thou didst waken me with the divine accents of Thy voice, and didst unveil to me Thy beauty, and didst enable me to listen to Thine utterances, and to recognize Thy Self, and to speak forth Thy praise, and to extol Thy virtues, and to be steadfast in Thy love."[2]

For many people, the most exhilarating facet of Bahá'u'lláh's role as the next Manifestation of God was the way He simultaneously fulfilled prophecies and expectations from all of the world's major religions. From the Bahá'í point of view, Bahá'u'lláh was the mystical return of Christ, ushering in the Day of Resurrection promised by the New Testament and the Qur'án. He was also the King of Glory mentioned in Psalms and awaited by Judaism. He was the tenth Avatar of Hinduism, the Shah Bahram or Saoshyant (Savior) of Zoroastrianism, and the Great Spirit anticipated by many American Indian tribes. He was also the Buddha Maitreye—the Buddha of universal fellowship. But, fascinating as it might be to investigate these claims, the primary goal of this chapter is to sketch out the genetic lines connecting Bahá'u'lláh to Abraham—which means it's time to take a look at the family tree.[3]

A COMPLICATED FAMILY

Bahá'u'lláh was a descendant of Abraham's third wife, Keturah. He was also a descendant of Sarah through the line of Isaac, Jacob, Jesse, and King David.[4]

The descent from Keturah is easy to understand. As described in chapter 17, Keturah's six sons spread out to the east of Canaan along various trade routes. Each son carried "gifts" from Abraham, and one of the most enduring was the gift of His genes. Because a major trade route ran though northern Iran, the genes might have reached that area within a century or so of Abraham's death. Or they could have filtered in later, through liaisons facilitated by invasions and counter-invasions among the various tribal nations of greater Mesopotamia. In either case, Bahá'u'lláh's ancestors, who came from northern Iran, carried the link, and every generation passed the heritage of Keturah along until, finally, it was inherited by the mother of Bahá'u'lláh.*

The descent from Sarah is much more complicated. It begins with a line leading back from Bahá'u'lláh's father to two of the twelve Sasanian kings who ruled Persia (including what is now Iran) for four centuries, from AD 224 to AD 636. From there, as laid out in a series of genealogical documents penned c. AD 900 by Muslim historian Muhammad Al-Tabari, it moves back to a man named Sasan, who was the grandfather of the first Sasanian king and gave his name to the dynasty of Sasanian kings.[5]

---

* In *God Passes By*, p. 94, Shoghi Effendi describes the lineage of Bahá'u'lláh, his great-grandfather, this way: "He derived His descent, on the one hand, from Abraham (the Father of the Faithful) through his wife Keturah, and on the other from Zoroaster, as well as from Yazdigird, the last king of the Sasaniyan dynasty." Because it was Bahá'u'lláh's father who was descended from Zoroaster and Yazdigird, the presumption I have made from Shoghi Effendi's wording is that it was Bahá'u'lláh's mother whose family traced its heritage to Katurah.

Sasan was born within a century or so of Jesus. He was a Zoroastrian priest and perhaps also a minor prince, but he is important here because according to Al-Tabari's genealogy, Sasan was a descendant of Cyrus the Great of Persia. Cyrus was a Zoroastrian and an empire-builder who raised an army, marched out of Persia and conquered Babylon in the sixth century BC. After adding the conquered lands to the Persian Empire, Cyrus did something so memorable that he is mentioned repeatedly in the Old Testament: he freed the Jews, who had been in Babylonian captivity for a half-century, and allowed them to return to Jerusalem to rebuild Solomon's temple.[6]

Al-Tabari indicates that while Cyrus was in Babylon, he took a Jewish woman named Rahab as a concubine. Rahab had a brother named Zerubbabel, and she asked Cyrus to appoint Zerubbabel as the leader of the exiles who were returning to Palestine. The appointment took place, and the Old Testament confirms that Zerubbabel left Babylon and moved to Jerusalem to lay the foundation of the second temple. Rahab, however, was content to stay with Cyrus, and she bore him a son named Sasan.

Naturally enough, Rahab shared Zerubbabel's genealogy, which is outlined in the Bible and clarified in the Bahá'í writings. Their line traces back through King David, through David's father, Jesse, and then to Jacob, to Isaac and, finally, to Sarah and Abraham.[7] In a genetic sense, then, Bahá'u'lláh "sits" on the throne of David, an attribute stressed in several Old Testament prophecies.

One last tidbit of information about Bahá'u'lláh's complicated genealogy is the information that He was also a descendant of Zoroaster. The first Sasanian king (Ardashir) was one of the hereditary guardians of a major Zoroastrian temple, a position indicating his descent from Zoroaster's children.[8] The succeeding Sasanian kings shared this link to Zoroaster, and thus Bahá'u'lláh did, too.

PRAISING THE PAST

Bahá'u'lláh frequently mentioned the Messengers of God Who preceded Him, and He praised Their accomplishments. He described Moses as the "Revealer of the Pentateuch," Who "held converse with God" and was "armed with the rod of celestial dominion." He wrote of Jesus as the "Spirit of God," and the "Author of the Gospel," Who came with "sovereignty and power."[9]

Muḥammad was described as a "Daystar of Truth," Whose Revelation was a trumpet call "sounded in the heart of the universe." Bahá'u'lláh also lauded the Báb, calling Him the "Primal Point" and the "Most Exalted One," whose countenance was so bright that it "hath enveloped, and will continue to envelop, the whole of creation."[10]

Bahá'u'lláh likened the previous Messengers to "Birds of the celestial Throne" who "all drink from the one Cup of the love of God," and proclaim the irresistible Faith of God. Although each Manifestation of God has a different personality, has been commissioned to reveal Himself though specific acts, bears a different name, and has a special mission, Bahá'u'lláh explained that all of them came in order "to liberate the children of men from the darkness of ignorance, and guide them to the light of true understanding."[11]

Bahá'u'lláh referred to Himself as a Voice, whose "sole purpose hath been to hand down unto men that which I was bidden to deliver by God . . .", and Whose objective was "the betterment of the world and the tranquility of its peoples."[12]

PARALLELS BETWEEN BAHÁ'U'LLÁH AND ABRAHAM

To mark Abraham's status as a Divine Messenger, God changed His birth name of *Abram* to *Abraham*, meaning *father of a multitude*. The same thing happened to Bahá'u'lláh, whose birth name of Mírzá Ḥusayn-'Alí was changed to *Bahá'u'lláh*, which means *Glory of God.*

Like Abraham, Bahá'u'lláh was banished more than once, and His final destination was the same: the Land of Canaan.

The first exile came in 1853, when the Persian government sent Bahá'u'lláh from Tehran in Persia to Baghdad, which at that time was under the rule of the Turkish Ottoman Empire. Although Baghdad had not yet been built when Abraham was alive, and

Abraham's birthplace lay in ruins by the time Bahá'u'lláh entered the world, the two cities were just miles apart, smack dab in the middle of Babylon or, as Genesis terms it, *Ur of the Chaldees.*

From Babylon / Ur / Mesopotamia, both Bahá'u'lláh and Abraham were banished to Turkey, and both of them were accompanied in their exile by family members. Constantinople (Istanbul) was the first Turkish city to which Bahá'u'lláh was sent. The exiles rode mules (women and children rode in *howdahs*—special seats strapped onto the backs of the mules), and the caravan was guarded by soldiers on horseback.

The thousand-mile journey from Baghdad to Constantinople took Bahá'u'lláh's party almost four months. The first half of the route ran along the Tigris River, paralleling the trek Abraham made along the Euphrates River during His move from Ur to Harran.

After three months in Constantinople, Bahá'u'lláh was sent to Adrianople (Edirne). Then, in 1868, He was exiled to the Land of Canaan (Palestine / Israel). He, His family, and a group of other Bahá'í prisoners—seventy people in all—were taken by boat from Gallipoli (Gelibolu) to Alexandria in Egypt (the land where Moses was born and that both Abraham and Jesus visited). From Alexandria, the boat sailed northwest to Canaan, landing at the prison of Acre. Acre is one of the oldest continuously-inhabited cities in the world, and it is quite possible Abraham, too, passed through Acre when going from Harran to Canaan.

There is no record of the prophecies that might have been fulfilled through the successive banishments of Abraham, but when pondering the exiles of Bahá'u'lláh, one can readily connect His movements with a biblical passage found in the Book of Micah: "In that day also he shall come even to thee from Assyria, and from the fortified cities, and from the fortress even to the river, and from sea to sea, and from mountain to mountain."[13]

Bahá'u'lláh came to the Land of Canaan by way of Baghdad (Assyria), and from the fortified cities of Constantinople and Adrianople. He was then confined to a fortress—the prison-fortress of

Acre. After two years in the fortress, He was released and allowed to live in the countryside near a stream. During that period, He was given the opportunity to make frequent visits to a quiet island in the stream, and a garden fragrant with the scent of jasmine and orange flowers was gradually created there. The island became known as the Riḍván Garden (Paradise Garden), and today it welcomes a steady flow of Bahá'í pilgrims.

"Sea to sea" matches the manner in which Bahá'u'lláh was forced to sail on the Black Sea, the Sea of Marmara, and then across the Mediterranean Sea to Acre. The final phrase of the verse in Micah—"mountain to mountain"—is an apt description of the way in which Bahá'u'lláh spent the early part of His life in the Alborz mountains of northern Iran, traveled into exile through the mountains of Iraq and Turkey, and then, near the end of His life, traveled around the bay from Acre to Haifa, Israel, where He pitched a tent and camped on the mountain whose name means *Vineyard of God*—Mount Carmel.*

---

* *Carmel* comes from the Hebrew term *Kerem-El,* which means *Vineyard of El* or *Vineyard of God.*

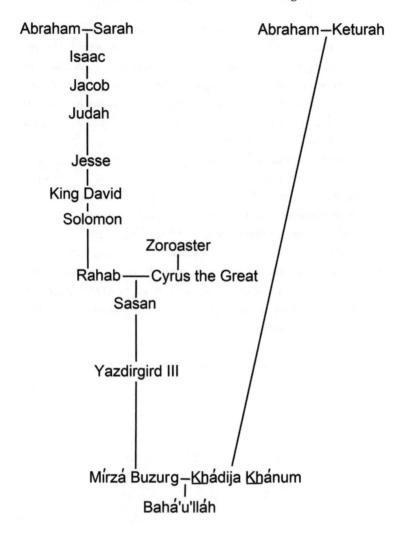

Simplified genealogy of Bahá'u'lláh

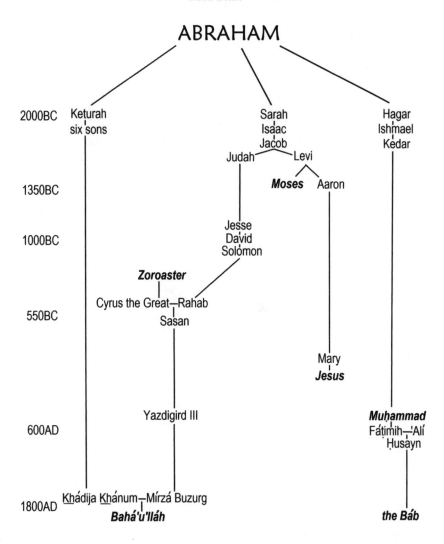

ABRAHAM

2000BC — Keturah / six sons — Sarah / Isaac / Jacob / Judah — Levi / Hagar / Ishmael / Kedar

Moses — Aaron

1350BC

Jesse / David / Solomon

1000BC

Zoroaster

Cyrus the Great—Rahab

Sasan

550BC

Mary / *Jesus*

Yazdigird III

Muḥammad / Fáṭimih—'Alí / Ḥusayn

600AD

Khádija Khánum—Mírzá Buzurg / *Bahá'u'lláh*

the Báb

1800AD

All of the genealogies plus a rough timeline

24

IDENTIFYING ABRAHAM'S DESCENDANTS

Know ye not why
We created you all from the same dust?
That no one should exalt himself over the other.
Bahá'u'lláh[1]

For millennia, each familial tribe, wherever it lived, was quite proud of itself. It drew pleasure and courage from the belief that it was distinctly different from other groups. The time it took to cover even short distances, coupled with the impossibility of quickly and easily crossing the largest oceans, reinforced this notion of separateness, as did differences in language, food, and customs. In spite of information contained in religious scriptures suggesting common ancestors, very few people were able to feel an intimate connection to someone hundreds or thousands of miles away whose name they did not know, whose picture they had never seen, and whose hand they were certainly never going to shake.

In the last five hundred years, however, the ways in which people create and define tribal loyalties have changed drastically, and they are continuing to change with every passing day. Many things have influenced the change, but the six that seem most important are communication, travel, tidal waves of emigration, widespread education, the emergence of the social sciences, and discoveries in the field of genetics. In exceedingly brief form, here's what has happened.

The first big jump in the field of communications came in the fifteenth century with the invention of metal presses containing reusable movable type. Within a hundred years, reliance on the tedious and expensive processes of block printing and hand-copying had ended in many countries, and inexpensive, mass-produced books began to flood the market. From there, methods of widespread communication advanced to newspapers (1605), then to telegraph (1844), then to telephone (1876), radio (1897), and television (1928). Right this minute, in the early years of the twenty-first century, communication is experiencing another intense growth spurt, this one due to the ubiquity of computers, cell phones, and the World Wide Web.

People have traveled hither and yon for millennia, but not very quickly. Land travel was by foot or on the back of an animal. Water transportation was limited to smallish boats powered by oars and / or sails. Most of them hugged the coastline for safety, though a few ventured across larger gaps. Boats large, sturdy, and fast enough to carry dozens of people plus heavy cargo back and forth across the enormous expanses of the Atlantic and Pacific Oceans are, like the printing press, a recent development. Only in the last five hundred years have we suddenly advanced from sailing ships, to steamships, to enormous oil-fired ocean liners with four thousand passengers, to trains, cars, airplanes, submarines, and space shuttles.

As a result of improved communications and better means of travel, wars and genocidal attacks were able to increase in size and range and, ironically, refugees from those conflicts were able to flee faster and further than ever before. Unprecedented waves of emigrants rendered homeless by violence or natural disasters began moving from country to country and even across oceans. The practice of taking indentured servants and slaves from country to country also added to the intercontinental mixing of people.

Improved communications and easy access to books and newspapers fostered the growth of literacy, which, in turn, spurred an increase in educational institutions. Wider travel produced explorers and journalists who published riveting descriptions of life in other places, and their reports were read by the increasingly large number of educated people. Curiosity about these alien peoples and places encouraged universities to establish departments of social sciences—anthropology, economics, linguistics, language, psychology, political science, and more. Researchers in the various social sciences began investigating why people do what they do, and humanity as a whole began to appreciate itself in ways unfathomable to its ancestors.

The scientific study of genetics sprouted in the mid-1800s. When, in the 1900s, it became possible to study genes at a molecular level, researchers suddenly realized that "Every drop of human blood contains a history book written in the language of our genes." The most recent genetic research reveals that modern man arose in Africa about two hundred thousand years ago, and that somewhere between forty thousand and seventy thousand years ago, a group of them left Africa and began trekking eastward. Slowly, so slowly that no one realized what was happening, the descendants of that group covered the world. It is only now, within the past two decades, that we—the divided tribes of man—have been faced with unequivocal scientific evidence that "All the variously shaped and shaded people of Earth trace their ancestry to African hunter-gatherers."[2]

One might conclude, on hearing about our relationship to ancient Africans, that each of us would be forced to trace our own family tree back for thirty or forty thousand years to produce a common ancestor. But, according to research done by Yale statistician Joseph Chang, writer Steve Olson, and computer-genealogist Mark Humprys, it's really not necessary to go back that far. The truth is much simpler: every single one of us has a common ancestor who lived just two or three thousand years ago. What's more, millions of pale-skinned Europeans and Americans have a much more recent and very surprising common ancestor: Muḥammad.[3]

When records of European ancestry are consulted and lines are followed for twenty generations or so, each line eventually claims the same person as an ancestor: a daughter of the Emir of Seville. The Emir, who lived c.1200, was a Muslim and a descendant of Muḥammad. His daughter, Theresa, who reportedly converted to Catholicism, married the King of Aragon, Alfonso IV. When this royal couple produced children, each one of them was, naturally enough, a descendant of Muḥammad.

Many of Theresa's descendants were members of Europe's royal families, including at least one king as well as a queen of Sicily. Royalty had better access to good food and water than the average person and, during the Middle Ages, could travel away from plague areas. These advantages often resulted in a higher-than-average survival rate. Combine those advantages with the predilection certain male members of royalty had for fathering children out of wedlock, and it's easy to see why contemporary Europeans whose families have lived in Europe for several centuries must count Theresa, the Emir of Seville, and Muḥammad as ancestors. And why, in both North and South America, descent from Muḥammad can be assumed by almost anyone whose family line traces back, on one side or another, to Europe.

FATHER ABRAHAM

When someone traces a family tree, the branches quickly become tangled in a forest of limbs rising from other family trees, creating a three-dimensional mess. My great-aunt turns out to be your grandmother. Your great-great grandfather from Boston, who captained a trading ship, managed to father an extra child while buying silk in China, which gives you some third cousins on the other side of the world. And so on. The numbers of each person's ancestors, writes Steve Olson, "are manageable in the first few generations—two parents, four grandparents, eight great-grandparents, sixteen great-great-grandparents—but they quickly spiral out of control. Go back forty generations, or about a thousand years, and each of us theoretically has more than a trillion direct ancestors—a figure that far exceeds the total number of human beings who have ever lived."[4]

Reconciling the notion of trillions of ancestors with the much smaller number of people who were actually alive is quite simple. With each step into the past, any individual's family tree is going to have more and more people in common with family trees of other people on the planet. "This means," writes Olson, "that the most recent common ancestor of all six billion people on earth today probably lived just a couple of thousand years ago. And not long before that the majority of the people on the planet were direct ancestors of everyone alive today. Confucius, Nefertiti, and just about any other ancient historical figure who was even moderately prolific must today be counted among everyone's ancestors."[5]

By adding a little something to the previous sentence without changing its validity, it is apparent that ***Abraham***, *Confucius, Nefertiti and just about any other ancient historical figure who was even moderately prolific must today be counted among everyone's ancestors.* If Abraham existed, and this book assumes He did, and if He had eight children, the number stated in Genesis, the obvious conclusion is that God's promise to Abraham has been abundantly fulfilled: "And I will make thy seed as the dust of the earth: so that if a man can number the dust of the earth, then shall thy seed also be numbered."[6]

Having reached the point of understanding that Abraham's seed has completely covered the earth, it's possible to conclude that God's promises about who will inherit the Land of Canaan have been fulfilled as well. No matter who legally owns any square foot of soil, he or she *must*, by the inexorable math of statistical genetics, be a descendant of not only Abraham but of all three of His wives. We have met the inheritors of the land, and they are us, no matter what we look like or what faith we follow.

There is also a second, even more literal sense in which Abraham's descendants have inherited the land of Canaan: All of His children—His religions—have important shrines and holy places in Israel. Every year thousands of pilgrims—each a seed of the Father of monotheism—journey to that special part of the earth, drawn by the unique role it has played in religious history.

IT WAS NEVER ABOUT GENEALOGY

The heart of Abraham's legacy seemed, for generations, to center on the importance of tribes and inheritance, but it's easy for modern eyes to perceive that DNA was never really essential to the story. Tracing hereditary lines was important only because people *believed* it was important. Abraham couldn't simply dismiss the tribal system that was already in place because people weren't ready to give it up, so He used the system as an incubator for monotheism. By connecting prophecies to the lineages, He reinforced the notion that it was important to pay close attention to spiritual matters, and He thereby strengthened the influence of religion.

But, even as Abraham indicated the importance of certain lineages, it was clear that the tradition of linking spiritual worthiness to ancestry must someday be outdated. When Abraham's seed covered the earth—or, to be more accurate, when science was at long last able to demonstrate that it had covered the earth—humankind would, happily or not, find itself united into a single worthy tribe, the tribe of Abraham.

The more one ponders genetics, the clearer it becomes that the simple lineages leading from Abraham to Moses, Jesus, Muḥammad, the Báb, and Bahá'u'lláh were never what they seemed to be. The deceptive straightforwardness of the lines was due partly to the widespread habit of tracing ancestry through fathers even though mothers were equal contributors, partly to the difficulties inherent in trying to keep track of every single line, partly to unrecorded liaisons, and partly to ignoring the effect of traders who trekked to foreign lands and begot children there.

The math of genetics produces a solid guess that Jesus might well have been a descendant of David, even though New Testament genealogies don't mention it and He didn't confirm it. The math

would indicate that Muḥammad and the Báb were, as claimed, descendants of Hagar, as well as being related to Sarah and Keturah.
The math would also bring to light something Bahá'u'lláh's parents
might have found astonishing: He, too, was descended from all
three of Abraham's wives.

The four-thousand-year-old legacy of Abraham is a convoluted
paradox of spiritual growth. The end of lineages was contained in
the beginning. Ancestry never really mattered, yet it was vital to
the story. The three wives came from dissimilar backgrounds and
led vastly different lives, but they became grandmothers to us all.
Abraham's seed spread out to cover the earth like dust, and we are
physically all made of that dust . . . the dusty DNA of our ancestors, the dust of Abraham, of Sarah, of Hagar, of Keturah, of Ishmael, Isaac, Zimran, Jokshan, Medan, Midian, Ishbak, and Shuah.

25

PROPHECY FULFILLED

There will be no peace among the nations
without peace among the religions.
There will be no peace among the religions
without dialogue among the religions.
Hans Kung[1]

In the time of Abraham, lineage almost always determined destiny because the world of humans was a world of distinct tribes made
up of people who were fairly closely related. Being born into Tribe
A rather than Tribe B determined who was friend and who was
foe. It generally controlled how you would make a living, where
you would reside, and what you would eat. It affected your name,
the language you spoke, the music you played, whom you married,
how your children would be educated (or not), and the way in
which you would be buried. And even if a tribe couldn't necessarily control the allegiances and yearnings of your inner soul, it did
dictate which gods you were expected to worship.

Refusing to accept the norms of the tribe could lead to banishment, and being exiled from the tribe into which you were born
was akin to being sentenced to death because it was not likely that
another tribe would want to adopt you. When Abraham was exiled
for opposing the beliefs of the prevailing tribe in Ur, and then ban-

ished a second time for not accepting the gods of His father's tribe, those who exiled Him hoped He would perish. What happened in Abraham's case, however, was that punishment turned into blessing because it became a pathway to a revolution in religious thought.

Through the process of moving to Canaan and starting a new tribe, Abraham was able to use the strength of tribal allegiance to create a religious culture quite different from that of other tribal groups. The followers of this new tribal faith took the idea of a single omnipotent God seriously, relinquished the worship of idols, and marked the uniqueness of their new beliefs through the ritual of circumcising baby boys. They celebrated links to their past by remembering that other spiritual giants, such as Enoch and Noah, were among their spiritual ancestors. And, as a bonus, they reveled in God's promise that Abraham's legacy—religious as well as genetic—would continue to be as important to the world in the future as it had in the past.

For about two thousand years, the monotheism of Abraham (and Moses) continued to be primarily an inherited religion belonging to a few special tribes. Within this protected environment, it was able to grow into a stable entity whose spiritual integrity and civilizing influence was noticed and appreciated by surrounding cultures. According to the Bahá'í writings, Hippocrates and Socrates were among the great thinkers who traveled from Greece to Canaan. While there, they "acquired wisdom from the Jewish prophets, studying the basis of ethics and morality, returning to their country with contributions which have made Greece famous."[2]

But, wonderful as it was that visitors from other regions could come to Israel and borrow ideas from monotheistic Judaism, it was difficult for these seekers of truth to be accepted by Judaism as legitimate followers of Moses and Abraham. One option for change, the easiest, was to marry a Jew, which guaranteed that the children of the marriage would be considered Jews by birthright. The other option involved two steps: The potential convert had to pledge allegiance not just to God, but also to the Jewish people. But, even after taking the pledge, the new convert wouldn't be considered a *real* Jew. Instead, he would have a sort of resident alien status and would be referred to as a *righteous proselyte*.[3] What these restrictions meant in practical terms was that monotheistic Judaism continued to be a religion in which membership was dictated by birth rather being a matter of choice, and the faith remained confined to a small area of the world.

In order for the monotheism of Abraham to spread to other countries, a new *modus operandi* was needed, something God supplied through the Revelation of Abraham's descendant, Jesus. Jesus did what had previously been unimaginable: He changed the definition of what a tribe could be by creating a spiritual clan in which DNA was irrelevant. Each member of the Christian tribe was linked to all of the other members—and to God—by mystical bonds of belief that were considered as powerful as ties of blood: "And looking at those who sat around him, he said, 'Here are my mother and my brothers! Whoever does the will of God is my brother and sister and mother.'"[4]

Jesus' revolutionary explanation that the spiritual connection between a person's heart and God was not necessarily tied to one's ancestors and didn't require loyalty to any particular familial tribe was not met with overwhelming enthusiasm, and He was crucified as a troublemaker. After Jesus' death, His brokenhearted disciples were absolutely astonished to find that their faith had not died with Him. Heartened by the realization that the new tribe—the tribe of Christianity—could be resurrected, could survive and flourish without the physical presence of its Founder, and without any genetic legacy from Him, the disciples set about the task of taking this expanded understanding of monotheism beyond the confines of Israel and into the wider world.

Muhammad continued what Jesus had begun by creating a third monotheistic Abrahamic tribe—Islam—and opening its doors to anyone who wished to enter. In addition, He confirmed the legitimacy of several other religions, including those formed solely by belief as well as those passed from generation to generation by blood ties. He mentioned a few of these religions by name, including Judaism and Christianity. The rest He covered by saying: "whoever submits his whole self to Allah and is a doer of good, he will get his reward with his Lord; on such shall be no fear, nor shall they grieve."[5]

Although there have been times and places when the first three religions of Abraham—Judaism, Christianity, and Islam—managed to reflect the spirit of love and respect shown by the Messengers of God who revealed them, the general tenor of the interactions among the three tribes for the last millenium has been one of fractiousness.

Like contentious siblings, various members of these three Abrahamic tribes have thought their own inheritance—spiritual or physical—to be better than that of the others, and each has yearned to believe itself the most beloved of God. Reading current newspapers, one is sometimes driven to despair by the feeling that such pride and hostility will continue forever. On the other hand, the story of Abraham contains a shimmering dewdrop of hope because it foreshadows a time when enmity will fade and a movement toward reconciliation will begin.

The prophetic foreshadowing of this religious reconciliation took place after the death of Abraham, when the two oldest sons, who had long been separated—Ishmael in Mecca and Isaac in Canaan—reunited. The two sons can be understood as representing the five Abrahamic faiths: Islam and the Bábí Faith through Ishmael; Judaism, Christianity, and the Bahá'í Faith through Isaac.

When Isaac and Ishmael met, they ignored their past differences and concentrated, instead, on doing something positive: they buried their father with love and dignity. This act of solidarity transmitted the clear and powerful message that their common descent from Abraham was more important than the fact that they had different mothers. A parallel process began in the religious communities of the world just over a century ago, and it has been picking up speed every since. The process is fraught with uncertainties, upheavals, and unpleasantness, but it is also dotted with delight, discovery, and determination—and it is happening everywhere.

MAKING PEACE

A willingness to investigate and honor the truths of other religions has, of course, never been entirely absent from human history. One early example of honoring a different belief system lies in
the way King Cyrus freed the Jews from Babylonian captivity and
allowed them to return to Jerusalem to rebuild their temple. But
in spite of individual examples like Cyrus, organized methods of
conducting amicable dialogues and widespread attempts at fostering interfaith friendships are a recent phenomenon.

The birth of international interfaith dialogue is generally agreed
to have occurred in 1893 when the first World's Parliament of Religions was held at the World Columbian Exposition in Chicago.
The Parliament, which lasted sixteen days, was attended by people
from many different countries, and it featured presentations on
numerous religions, including Judaism, Christianity, Islam, Hinduism, and Buddhism, as well as Zoroastrianism and Shintoism.
The Bahá'í Faith was introduced, Mary Baker Eddy gave a lecture
on Christian Science, Swami Vivekananda spoke about Hinduism,
and there was much, much more.[6]

In a closing statement, Mr. C. C. Bonney, who had served
as President of all of the Congresses held during the Parliament,
summed up the aspirations of the group by saying:

> The wonderful success of this first actual Congress of the
> Religions of the world is the realization of a conviction which
> has held my heart for many years. I became acquainted with
> the great religious systems of the world in my youth, and have
> enjoyed an intimate association with leaders of many churches
> during my mature years. I was thus led to believe that if the
> great religious truths could be brought into relations of friend-
> ly intercourse, many points of sympathy and union would be
> found, and the coming unity of mankind in the love of God
> and the service of many be greatly facilitated and advanced.
>
> What many men deemed impossible God has finally wrought.
> The religions of the world have actually met in a great and

imposing assembly; they have conferred together on the vital questions of life and immortality in a frank and friendly spirit, and now they part in peace with many warm expressions of mutual affection and respect . . .

The influence which this Congress of the Religions of the World will exert on the peace and prosperity of the world is beyond the power of human language to describe. For this influence, borne by those who have attended the sessions of the Parliament of Religions to all parts of the earth, will affect in some important degree all races of men, all forms of religions, and even all governments and social institutions.[7]

The Parliament did not have any kind of follow-up meeting or forum, and in the first few decades after the Columbian Exposition, when the world was overtaken by World Wars I and II, it was all too easy to assume that the event had achieved nothing. But now, more than a hundred years later, the influence of the Parliament is evident in the astounding number of organizations that have arisen to promote interfaith dialogue and understanding. Some, like the United Religions Initiative, and the annual World Interfaith Harmony Week promoted by the United Nations, are global; others, such as the Interfaith Network for the United Kingdom, the North American Interfaith Network, and the Ethiopian Interfaith Peacebuilding Initiative, cover anything from a single country to a whole continent. And a few are devoted specifically to two or more of the Abrahamic faiths, including the Abrahamic Interfaith Dialogue Society of Istanbul.

Thousands of local interfaith initiatives have given birth to youth groups, books clubs, discussion groups, festivals, forums, and citywide councils, such as the Kharagpur Peace Circle in West Bengal, the Interfaith Forum in Greenville, South Carolina, and the NCRR (Nikkei for Civil Rights & Redress) coalition in Tokyo that sponsors an interfaith dinner during Ramadan. Interfaith calendars have been created, interfaith bumper stickers can be spotted on passing cars, and the Internet is bursting with sites offering the sacred texts of just about any nameable religion, as well as questions and answers about various religious customs, lists of holy days, overviews of different faiths, blogs on what daily life is like for individual believers, and columns of advice on how to form and conduct an interfaith group of one's own.

What's more, the Parliament of Religions has been revived. A centenary meeting was held in Chicago in 1993, and it has been followed by a series of gatherings spaced five years apart. Each meeting has been in a different venue, ranging from Cape Town to Barcelona to Mexico City to Melbourne, and each one has drawn thousands of attendees.

Wherever and whenever these interfaith events take place, one can symbolically watch Isaac happily thumping Ishmael on the shoulder or Hagar hugging Sarah and Keturah. And, based on the best models of how DNA has been passed around the world in the last forty centuries, one can perceive a trace of Abraham in each and every face.

APPENDIX A

BUT WHAT ABOUT
OTHER RELIGIONS?

Man must be a lover of the light
no matter from what dayspring it may appear.
He must be a lover of the rose
no matter in what soil it may be growing.
He must be a seeker of the truth
no matter from what source it comes.
Attachment to the lantern is not loving the light.
'Abdu'l-Bahá[1]

This book has focused on five Abrahamic faiths, but it does not in any way seek to overlook the other religions of the world or deny their validity. Just the opposite. Jesus certainly hinted at the soundness of other faiths by saying "And other sheep I have not of this fold." [2] Muḥammad carefully affirmed the divine origin of several revelations besides that of Islam, and Bahá'u'lláh declared the authenticity of many religions. The Bahá'í writings contain references to Zoroastrianism, Buddhism, and Hinduism, along with Judaism, Christianity, and Islam. There are a multitude of marvelous statements that could be made about the history and teachings of the Messengers of God Who have appeared outside of the Abrahamic cycle, but the most natural question to consider within the context of this book is: Are there any genetic connections between Abraham and Hinduism, Zoroastrianism, or Buddhism?

Unfortunately, none of the world's sacred scriptures provides any sort of clear-cut answer to this question. And neither do any historical documents. If genealogies straightforwardly connecting these religions to Abraham were ever recorded or passed along as oral traditions, they either haven't yet come to light or haven't survived the depredations of history. Nevertheless, there has been plenty of speculation.

HINDUISM

Discussing Hinduism is a complicated endeavor, beginning with its very name—a name often used quite indiscriminately to mean any number of traditions, philosophies, and religions that are directly connected to the Indian subcontinent. In the beginning, though, the term *Hindu* had nothing to do with religion but was simply the Persian term for the Sindhu river, which lay to the east of Persia. As the word jumped from language to language, *Hindu* began being used to refer to the people in that area and to their religion while the river's name changed to the one we use today, Indus, and the country where the river lay became known as India.

When dealing with the subject of Abraham, it is not the widest spectrum of Hinduism that concerns us but, rather, the name of the central deity of the religion as it was practiced in ancient times by the people who lived along the Hindu / Indus River. The deity was *Brahma,* and the priests who conducted the rites associated with his worship were *Brahmans.* The linguistic similarity between *Brahma* and *Abraham* is so obvious that it has become the base on which a great many theories about their relationship have been built. Let's look at two of them.

A cursory summary of the first theory (which we could call the Judeo-Christian approach if we wanted to) includes these ideas: The similarity between Abraham and Brahma must mean that this branch of Hinduism, often called Brahmanism, is connected to Abraham through one or more of Keturah's sons. Abraham sent these six sons to the east, and they carried His religion with them.

They—or their descendants—eventually taught it to the people along the Sindu / Hindu / Indus river.

The religion changed over the years, acquiring new features and dropping out some old ones, including the fact that Abraham was the true originator of the religion, but His name remained emblazoned upon it, albeit in a slightly altered form. Other traces of the relationship can be detected here and there, such as the name of one of the Hindu goddesses—Saraswati—which is strangely similar to Abraham's first wife, Sarai / Sarah. And, as the cherry on the sundae, there exists a tantalizing report from a seventeenth-century missionary, Phillipus Baldeus: While living in Sri Lanka, Baldeus met a family of Brahmans who told him that their ancestors were descendants of Keturah.[3]

Moving from theory A to theory B (which might best be characterized as the Brahmanistic or Hindu side), we find arguments that are essentially the same. Or, more accurately, they are the same except for a small but very significant disagreement about who came first. Side B begins with the notion that Abraham was not a forefather of Brahmanism but a descendant of it. From this point of view, Abraham's ancestors were forced out of the Indian subcontinent by a devastating famine, whereupon they moved westward into Mesopotamia and settled in Ur of the Chaldees. When Abraham was born, His parents named Him in honor of their ancestral god of creation, Brahma. One writer, Prithvi Vinod, sums it up like this:

> Jews are none other than Yadavas [an Indian clan] who migrated from India after the great drought of 2200 BC which led to the drying up of the Saraswati River. It has already been pointed out by several historians that Abraham of Jews and Brahma of Hindus are too close by name to miss. Additionally Sarai is too close to the Hindu goddess Saraswati, the wife of Brahma. And as in Hindu legends, Abraham along with Sarai fathers a large number of nations across the world.

Mount Moriah [where Abraham intended to sacrifice His son] is pointed out to be Mount Meru of the Hindus.

Abraham's son Isaac is none other than Iswar a.k.a. Shiva [Hindu deity of transformation]. In Hindu legends, Iswar is the son of Brahma; he is even called Brahmaputra, meaning son of Brahma.

Rebekah, the wife of Isaac, is none other than Ambica, the wife of Shiva. Ambika / Rebekah—the names are quite similar. Rebekah of Jews is portrayed as a pleasing and benign woman, and, just like in Judaism, the Ambika of Hindus is actually a benign and pleasing goddess. And what does the son Ishmael of Hagar signify? Ishmael is just a morphed form of Ishalay (Isha + Alay) meaning temple of Ishwar or Shiva.[4]

Vinod also connects Abraham's second wife, Keturah, directly to the Hindu goddess Gayatri. And he believes, by dint of linguistic analysis, that the six sons of Abraham through Keturah "are none other than the Vedic gods of India . . . Zimran is Devendra, Zokshan is Daksha, Medan is Marut, Midian is Mithra, Ishbak is Aswins and Shuah is Rudra."[5]

The congruence of so many Brahmanic / Abrahamic names is endlessly fascinating, pushing us to conclude that there must be a relationship—genetic, theological, or both—between the religions, even though many of the details remain murky.

ZOROASTER

Zoroaster was probably born c. 700 BC, give or take a century or two. He spent most—maybe all—of His life in Persia and was the Founder of Zoroastrianism. The priests of that religion were known as Magi, the very same Magi or Wise Men mentioned in the New Testament, the ones who employed painstakingly precise astronomical observations to guide them to the birthplace of Jesus.

In linking Zoroaster to Abraham, Jewish academician Jacob Neusner notes the existence of several claims in centuries-old Jewish sources, as well as the writings of Armenian-Christians, that

Persians (which, by implication, includes Zoroaster) were "children of Keturah." The Bahá'í writings also place some of Keturah's sons in Persia but do not mention a direct connection to Zoroaster.[6]

Whether any formal genealogical connection can be verified or not, the math of genetics would assign a reasonable probability to Zoroaster's chances of being able to claim Abraham as a forefather. They were separated by a thousand years or so, plenty long enough for Abraham's DNA to connect with at least one of Zoroaster's many ancestors.

BUDDHA

Buddha was born c. 600 BC (some historians place the date nearer 400 BC) in Nepal. He is only rarely linked to Abraham, perhaps because the general concept of genealogies has never been especially important in Buddhism. The few family trees that exist for Buddha were not constructed until centuries after His death, and they are usually thought of as being more symbolic than literal.

Another reason for ignoring Buddha's ancestry lies in the way that He, like Jesus, is not considered to have been the product of sexual intercourse. He is described as having chosen his mother— The Lady Maya Diva—and incarnating himself into her, which makes him a descendant of no one except God.[7] Nevertheless, should one wish to employ the math of genetics when considering the heritage of Buddha's mother, there was more than enough time between Abraham and Buddha for the essential DNA to work its way from Canaan to Nepal.

APPENDIX B

THE ANCIENT SABEAN FAITH AND SABEANISM TODAY

Great is thy name, my Lord.
I mention your name with pure heart, thou Lord of all worlds;
Blessed and Holy thy name my Lord, the High the Mighty,
King of Worlds of Sublime Light,
whose power is infinite thou, the brilliant and the inexhaustible Light.
God, you, the Merciful, the compassionate,
and the Forgiving the Savior of all believers
and the supporter of all good people.
Thou art the wise, the omnipotent who knows everything.
Thou art capable of doing every thing;
Lord of all worlds of Light, the high, middle and lower worlds.
Thou art of the respectful Face, which cannot be seen;
thou art the only God who has no partner and no equal in his Power.
Any one who trusts in you will never be let down;
any one who recites your name will never be disappointed;
any one who depends on you will never be humiliated,
Lord of all angels, without His presence, there is no existence;
without Him, nothing could exist,
He is Eternal without beginning and an end.
Sabean-Mandaean prayer[1]

As mentioned in chapter 2, Abraham was a member of the Sabean Faith (alternate spellings are *Sabaean* and *Sabian*) before He realized His destiny as a Messenger of God. Regrettably, for those of us who want to know more about Sabeanism, untangling the convoluted skein of its history produces more questions than answers. As one frustrated Englishman concluded, "Among the various problems that have vexed the souls of learned men, few have provoked greater controversy, or given rise to more fanciful and conflicting theories, than that connected with the name of Sabian . . . To write the history of the numerous significations which have been attached to the word Sabian is to chronicle the errors of the learned world . . ."[2] Taking these words to heart, I have listed below a tiny fraction of what is known or conjectured.

- In the Bahá'í writings, Shoghi Effendi provides three pieces of information about the Sabean Faith: Its Founder is considered to have been a divinely-sent Messenger. Abraham is thought to have been a follower of Sabeanism. The country where the religion became widespread and flourished was Chaldea [i.e. Ur of the Chaldees].[3]

- The interconnectedness of many of the belief systems of the ancient world is being increasingly confirmed by archaeological discoveries. In 2007, *Science Magazine* reported that "The scatter of high-priced trade goods, seals, and pottery has revealed the existence of networks linking Middle Asia's urban centers with each other and with Mesopotamia and the Indus." In addition to items of trade, certain forms of religion seem to have been shared by the urban centers of the Middle East and the Indus Valley in the centuries prior to Abraham. The evidence, *Science* reports, lies in "Massive ceremonial platforms," often called ziggurats, "whose remains are plentiful in both Mesopotamia and Afghanistan." Amid the ruins of the large city of Mohenjo-Daro (in southern Pakistan, along the Indus River), a central structure "long thought to be the remains of a later Buddhist stupa, may be a platform like those built to the west, says Giovanni Veradi of the University of Naples." This interconnectedness raises the possibility that most of the ziggurats of the ancient world, and perhaps even the pyramids of Egypt, were inspired by Sabeanism.[4]

- The Old Testament contains three references to Sabeans, but each seems to indicate a different group of people: one group in Arabia, a second in Ur of the Chaldees, and a third in Africa, perhaps in the area of Ethiopia. The manner in which any of them might have been connected to the others isn't clear.

- Three verses of the Qur'án (2:62, 5:69, and 22:17) mention Sabeans as having a valid religion. Early Muslims, however, were not absolutely certain to whom they should apply the label, and Islamic literature contains several different descriptions of who the Sabeans really were. In AD 830, a group of people in Harran, Turkey, who worshipped the moon god, Sin, claimed to be the Sabeans of the Qur'án and were granted that status, but it has been suggested that they did it primarily to avoid converting to Islam (see chapter 5 of this book).

- One understanding of why Muḥammad referred to *Sabaeans* even though His followers were not familiar with that term is that He was being purposely ambiguous. From this point of view, He was deliberately encouraging tolerance toward other religions, wherever and whatever they might be.

- Several groups of people known as Sabeans, Sabean-Mandaeans, or simply Mandaeans exist today. They connect their beliefs to a number of prophets and Messengers of the past, including Seth, Enoch, Noah, Abraham, and, usually, St. John the Baptist. Many people believe the Mandaeans are the remnants of what was originally the Sabean Faith as mentioned by Muḥammad, but that it is now impossible to discern the original teachings because the faith has changed so extensively over the course of several millennia. Until recently, the preponderance of Sabean-

Mandaeans lived in Iraq, but intense persecution has forced most of them to emigrate. For further information on the Sabean-Mandaeans, check these Web sites: Mandaean Root.com, http://www.mandaeanroot.com/; Mandaean Associations Union, http://www.mandaeanunion.com/; Radio Free Europe / Radio Liberty, http://www.rferl.org/.

NOTES

1 / ON THE MOVE

1. Qur'án 26:69 (Rodwell translation).
2. 'Abdu'l-Bahá, *Some Answered Questions*, p. 12; Genesis 11:28–31 (King James Version and New International Version).
3. Joshua 24:3 (King James Version).
4. Distance of Kutha from Baghdad based on coordinates of 32° 44'N, 44°40'E and calculated using Google Earth.
5. Bahá'u'lláh, The Kitáb-i-Iqán, ¶67.
6. Ginzburg, *The Legends of the Jews*, p. 186.
7. Curatola, *The Art and Architecture of Mesopotamia*, pp. 27–28.
8. Genesis 9:20–29 (New Revised Standard Version).
9. *The Paul Revere House*, http://www.paulreverehouse.org/bio/silvershop.shtml.
10. Smith, *The Holy Bible: Containing the Old and New Testaments*, Psalms 78:2.
11. Psalms 78:2 (King James Version).
12. Mark 4:33–34 (New International Version); Qur'án 24:35 (Pickthall); Bahá'u'lláh, *Tablets of Bahá'u'lláh revealed after the Kitáb-i-Aqdas*, p. 173.
13. Isaiah 5:7 (King James Version).
14. John 15:1 (King James Version).
15. Psalms 60:3 (American King James Version).
16. Bahá'u'lláh, *The Summons of the Lord of Hosts*, "Lawḥ-i-Ra'ís," ¶8.
17. Bahá'u'lláh, *Prayers and Meditations*, p. 103.
18. II Corinthians 5:1–4 (New International Version).

2 / A RISING STAR

1. Job 38:32 (World English Bible).
2. Bahá'u'lláh, The Kitáb-i-Iqán, ¶67.
3. Rolleston, *Mazzaroth; or, the Constellations*, part I, p. 3.

4. Ibid., part II, pp. 10, 22, 23.
5. Jewish tradition gives *Emtelai* as the name of Abraham's mother, as noted in Ginzberg, *The Legends of the Jews*, pp. 186–87.
6. Nemet-Najat, Daily Life in Ancient Mesopotamia, p. 129.
7. Ibid.
8. Ginzburg, *The Legends of the Jews*, p. 210.
9. Ibid.

3 / INTO THE FIRE

1. Qur'án 36:30, quoted in Bahá'u'lláh, *The Summons of the Lord of Hosts*, "Súriy-i-Haykal," ¶242.
2. The story and dialogue are based on accounts in two books: Baring-Gould, *Legends of the Patriarchs and Prophets and Other Old Testament Characters from Various Sources*, pp. 156–57, and Ginzburg, *The Legends of the Jews*, pp. 196, 214.
3. Shoghi Effendi, *The Promised Day Is Come*, ¶291.
4. Ginzburg, *The Legends of the Jews*, pp. 196–97.
5. Dialogue based on information in two books: Vermes, *Post-biblical Jewish Studies*, pp. 160–61, and Bialik, *Sefer Ha-Aggadah: The Book of Jewish Folklore and Legend*, p. 32.
6. Qur'án 37:95 and 21:68–69 (Palmer translation).
7. Bahá'u'lláh, The Kitáb-i-Íqán, ¶11.
8. 'Abdu'l-Bahá, *The Promulgation of Universal Peace: Talks Delivered by 'Abdu'l-Bahá during His Visit to the United States and Canada in 1912*, p. 561.
9. Ibid., p. 511.

4 / EXILE

1. Bahá'u'lláh, *Prayers and Meditations*, p. 308.
2. Momen, *A Basic Bahá'í Dictionary*, pp. 144–45.
3. Bahá'u'lláh, Epistle to the Son of the Wolf, p. 22.
4. Qur'án 6:75 (Pickthall translation).
5. From Ginzburg, *The Legends of the Jews*, p. 199.
6. 'Abdu'l-Bahá, *The Promulgation of Universal Peace: Talks Delivered by 'Abdu'l-Bahá during His Visit to the United States and Canada in 1912*, p. 516.

7. Ibid.
8. Ginzburg, *The Legends of the Jews*, p. 201.
9. Transportation information gleaned from Lawler, "Middle Asia Takes Center Stage," p. 588; Scarre, *Smithsonian Timelines of the Ancient World*, p. 176; and Bulliet, *The Camel and the Wheel*, p. 56.
10. Spencer, "The Marsh Arabs Revisited," p. 32.
11. "In the Marshes of Iraq," http://www.saudiaramcoworld.com/issue/196606/in.the.marshes.of.iraq.htm.
12. Ammianus Marcellinus, quoted in Green, *The City of the Moon God: Religious Traditions of Harran*, p. 1.
13. Green, *The City of the Moon God: Religious Traditions of Harran*, p. 19.

5 / THREAT AND PROMISE

1. Genesis 11:32 (New International Version).
2. "The Beehive Enigma," http://www.saudiaramcoworld.com/issue/196706/the.beehive.enigma.htm.
3. Ibid.
4. Green, *The City of the Moon God: Religious Traditions of Harran*, pp. 27, 216, 4; Lloyd and Brice, "Harran," p. 95. See Appendix B for more information on the Sabian / Sabean religion.
5. Lloyd and Brice, "Harran," p. 83; Lawrence, *The Diary Kept by T. E. Lawrence While Travelling in Arabia During 1911*, pp. 8–9.
6. Lloyd and Brice, "Harran," p. 83.
7. Szulc, "Journey of Faith," p. 3, http://ngm.nationalgeographic.com/features/world/asia/israel/abraham-text/1.
8. Jenkins, *The Cambridge History of Western Textiles*, p. 43.
9. Klinghoffer, *The Discovery of God*, p. 31.
10. 'Abdu'l-Bahá, *Some Answered Questions*, p. 12.
11. Qur'án 19:43–46 (Rodwell translation).
12. Ibid., 19:47.
13. Ibid., 19:48.
14. Ibid., 19:49.
15. Genesis 12:1–3 (New International Version).
16. Matthew 7:26–27 (New American Standard Bible).
17. Job 4:8–9 (King James Version).

18. Bahá'u'lláh, The Hidden Words, Arabic no. 5.
19. Holley, *Bahai: The Spirit of the Age*, p. 100.
20. Luke 9:60 (King James Version).
21. 'Abdu'l-Bahá, *Some Answered Questions*, p. 12.

6 / ON THE ROAD AGAIN

1. Thomas Huxley, cited in Evans, *Dictionary of Quotations*, p. 711.
2. 'Abdu'l-Bahá, *Selections from the Writings of 'Abdu'l-Bahá*, no. 222.2.
3. John 4:1 (King James Version); Shoghi Effendi, *Arohanui*, p. 94.
4. Young, "A Mathematical Approach to Certain Dynastic Spans in the Sumerian King List," pp. 123–29.
5. Harris, *Gender and Aging in Mesopotamia: The Gilgamesh Epic and Other Ancient Literature*, pp. 3, 30.
6. Conacher and Sala, *Land Degradation in Mediterranean Environments of the World*, p. 251; Dumper et al., *Cities of the Middle East and North Africa: A Historical Encyclopedia*, p. 4.

7 / THE LAND OF CANAAN

1. Fuller, cited in Evans, *A Psychoanalytic History of the Jews*, p. 705.
2. Hillel, *The Natural History of the Bible*, p. 17.
3. Finklestein and Silberman, *The Bible Unearthed*, p. 319.
4. Qur'án 11:41–44, p. 129 (Turner translation).
5. 'Abdu'l-Bahá, *Some Answered Questions*, p. 213.
6. Leeming, *Jealous Gods and Chosen People*, p. 38; Horowitz, *Mesopotamian Cosmic Geography*, p. 10.
7. Shoghi Effendi, *The Promised Day is Come*, ¶291; Oden, "The Persistence of Canaanite Religion," p. 31; Becking et al., *Only One God? Monotheism in Ancient Israel and the Veneration of the Goddess Asherah*, p. 25; Falk, *A Psychoanalytic History of the Jews*, p. 48.
8. Scharfstein, *Torah and Commentary*, p. 43; Plaut et al., *The Torah: A Modern Commentary*, pp. 96, 100, 306; Elwell and Comfort, *Tyndale Bible Dictionary*, p. 542; Horowitz, *Mesopotamian Cosmic Geography*, p. 107.
9. Deiss and Beaumont, *Joseph, Mary, Jesus*, pp. 8–13.
10. Henry, *God, Revelation, and Authority*, pp. 182–83.

11. Exodus 20:3–4 (New International Version).
12. Acts 19:26 (New Living Translation).
13. Genesis 12:8 (King James Version).

8 / A LESSON FOR PHARAOH

1. Qur'án 3:8 (Turner translation).
2. Genesis 12:10 (New American Standard Bible).
3. Swedenborg, *The Apocalypse Explained According to the Spiritual Sense*, pp. 806–7.
4. Amos 8:11 (King James Version).
5. John 6:35 (New American Standard Bible).
6. Qur'án 106:3–4 (Pickthall translation).
7. 'Abdu'l-Bahá, *Selections from the Writings of 'Abdu'l-Bahá*, no. 190.2.
8. Hillel, *The Natural History of the Bible*, p. 60.
9. Genesis 12:11–13 (King James Version).
10. Strouhal and Forman, *Life of the Ancient Egyptians*, pp. 54–55.
11. Genesis 12:18–19 (New International Version).
12. Shoghi Effendi, *Dawn of a New Day*, p. 197.
13. Matthew 12:50 (King James Version); Qur'án 49:10 (Palmer and also Yusuf Ali translations).
14. Bukhari, *The Hadith of Bukhari*, 3:34:420.
15. Ibid., 3:34:420, 4:55:578, and 3:47:803.
16. I Kings 8:38 (King James Version).
17. Genesis Rabbah 45:1, cited in Wiesel, *Wise Men and Their Tales: Portraits of Biblical, Talmudic, and Hasidic Masters*, p. 14.

9 / THE APOSTLE IN SODOM

1. The Qur'án, Sura 37 (Palmer translation).
2. Genesis 13:5–9 (King James Version).
3. Psalms 78:52 (King James Version).
4. Genesis 13:10 (New International Version).
5. Genesis 2:9 (New International Version); Collinson et al., *Fifty Eastern Thinkers*, p. 4. Tradition, as cited in this book, states that Zoroaster was initially reviled, later found favor with a ruler who promoted His teachings, and then was murdered while praying.

6. Genesis 13:13 (King James Version).
7. Genesis 14:22–23 (New Living Translation).
8. Genesis 14:19 (New International Version).
9. Genesis 14:18 (King James Version) and Hebrews 7:2 (New American Standard Bible).
10. Hebrews 7:15–17 (New American Standard Bible).
11. Osborne and Comfort, *Life Application Bible Commentary: Hebrews*, p. 95.

10 / PROMISES, PROMISES

1. Qur'án 3:9 (Palmer translation).
2. Genesis 13:16 (King James Version); Genesis 15:4 (King James Version and New American Standard Bible).
3. Genesis 15:9 (New International Version).
4. 'Abdu'l-Bahá, *The Promulgation of Universal Peace: Talks Delivered by 'Abdu'l-Bahá during His Visit to the United States and Canada in 1912*, p. 635.
5. King and Stager, *Life in Biblical Israel*, p. 44.
6. Silver, *History of Messianic Speculation in Israel*, p. 38; Gonen, *Burial Patterns and Cultural Diversity in Bronze-Age Canaan*, p. 4.
7. Genesis 15:13–16 (King James Version).
8. Miller and Hayes, *A History of Ancient Israel and Judah*, p. 38.
9. Genesis 15:17 (New International Version).
10. Genesis 15:18 (New American Standard Bible).

11 / ASTONISHED BY AN ANGEL

1. Thoreau, *Walden and Other Writings of Henry David Thoreau*, p. 77.
2. Genesis 16:1 (New International Version).
3. Genesis 16:2 (King James Version).
4. Ginzburg, *The Legends of the Jews*, p. 238.
5. Genesis 16:7–9 (King James Version).
6. Luke 24:23 (New Revised Standard Version); Numbers 22:31 (New Revised Standard Version); 'Abdu'l-Bahá, *Selections from the Writings of 'Abdu'l-Bahá*, no. 39.3.
7. Genesis 16:9 (King James Version).

8. Genesis 16:11 (American King James Version).

9. Genesis 16:10 (New Revised Standard Version).

10. Genesis 16:12 (New American Standard Bible).

11. Genesis 16:12 (American King James Version).

12. Genesis 16:12 (New International Version).

13. Alter, *The Five Books of Moses: A Translation with Commentary*, p. 80.

14. Mir, *Understanding the Islamic Scripture: A Study of Selected Passages from the Qur'án*, p. 34.

15. Maalouf, *Arabs in the Shadow of Israel*, p. 73.

16. Genesis 16:13 (World English Bible).

17. Genesis 16:13 (World English Bible and Young's Literal Translation of the Bible).

12 / THE SECOND HEIR

1. Blanchard, cited in Bliss, *The World's Best Poetry*, p. 37.

2. Genesis 17:16 (King James Version).

3. Freedman et al., *Eerdmans Dictionary of the Bible*, p. 9.

4. Cook, *The Holy Bible, According to the Authorized Version (AD 1611)*, p. 120; 'Abdu'l-Bahá, *The Promulgation of Universal Peace: Talks Delivered by 'Abdu'l-Bahá during His Visit to the United States and Canada in 1912*, p. 243.

5. Genesis 17:2–8 (New Living Translation).

6. Genesis 17:2–8 (King James Version).

7. Genesis 17:18 (King James Version and New International Version).

8. Genesis 17:20 (King James Version); Genesis 17:21 (New American Standard Bible); Genesis 17:19 (King James Version).

9. Genesis 17:23–25 (King James Version).

10. Gollaher, *Circumcision: A History of the World's Most Controversial Surgery*, p. 1.

11. Denniston et al., *Male and Female Circumcision: Medical, Legal, and Ethical Considerations in Pediatric Practice*, p. 145.

12. Jeremiah 4:4 (King James Version); Colossians 2:11 (New International Version).

13. American Urological Association, http://urologyhealth.org/pediatric/index.cfm?cat=10&topic=350.

14. Task Force on Circumcision, *Circumcision Policy Statement,* pp. 686–93.
15. Genesis 18:1–2 (King James Version). The final sentence is from the New International Version.
16. Saxon, *The Eucharist in Romanesque France: Iconography and Theology,* p. 184.
17. Sheridan, *Genesis 12–50,* pp. 62–63.

13 / ANGELS IN SODOM

1. "All Through the Night" (Old Welsh Folksong). Lyrics from http://ingeb.org/songs/sleepmyc.html.
2. Genesis 18:23–35 (New Living Translation).
3. Genesis 19:1–14 (New Revised Standard Version).
4. Genesis 19:25 (New Living Translation); Qur'án 53:53–54 (Yusuf Ali translation).
5. Enzel et al., *New Frontiers in Dead Sea Paleoenvironmental Research,* p. 9.
6. Rapp, *Archaeomineralogy,* p. 236.
7. Genesis 19:28 (New Living Translation).
8. Matthew 5:13 (King James Version); 'Abdu'l-Bahá, *The Promulgation of Universal Peace: Talks Delivered by 'Abdu'l-Bahá during His Visit to the United States and Canada in 1912,* pp. 215–16; Colossians 4:6 (New American Standard Bible).
9. Qur'án 35:13 and 55:19–22 (Rodwell translation).
10. Bahá'u'lláh, The Kitáb-i-Íqán, ¶111.

14 / DYING OF THIRST

1. Shurcliff, *A Man Walks the Earth: Near and Far in New England,* p. 61.
2. Genesis 21:6 (New Revised Standard Version); Qur'án 14:39 (Palmer translation).
3. Genesis 21:10 (New American Standard Bible).
4. Genesis 21:12–13 (King James Version).
5. Genesis 21:14 (New International Version).
6. Lings, *Muhammad: His Life Based on the Earliest Sources,* p. 2; Bukhari, *The Hadith of Bukhari,* 4:55:583.
7. Qur'án 14:37 (Yusuf Ali translation).

8. Genesis 21:15–16 (New International Version).
9. Bukhari, *The Hadith of Bukhari*, 3:55:583; Darr, Shaheen. "The miracle of Zam Zam water." http://www.helium.com/ items/1052721-the-miracle-of-zam-zam-water.
10. Genesis 21:18–20 (King James Version).
11. Genesis 21:20–21 (King James Version).
12. 'Abdu'l-Bahá, *Selections from the Writings of 'Abdu'l-Bahá*, no. 210.5; Qur'án 19:55 (Yusuf Ali).
13. Elwell and Comfort, *Tyndale Bible Dictionary*, p. 429; Shoghi Effendi, *Letters from the Guardian to Australia and New Zealand*, p. 41.
14. Lings, *Muḥammad: His Life Based on the Earliest Sources*, p. 4.
15. Psalms 84:3–6 (New Living Translation).
16. Qur'án 3:90–91 (Rodwell translation).
17. Lings, *Muḥammad: His Life Based on the Earliest Sources*, p. 4; Balyuzi, *Muḥammad and the Course of Islam*, p. 13.
18. Lings, *Muḥammad: His Life Based on the Earliest Sources*, p. 5; Balyuzi, *Muḥammad and the Course of Islam*, p. 133.

15 / THE MYSTERY OF SACRIFICE

1. James 2:21–22 (New International Version).
2. Genesis 22:2 (New American Standard Bible).
3. Qur'án Sura 37 (Palmer translation); Bahá'u'lláh, *Gleanings from the Writings of Bahá'u'lláh*, no. 32.1.
4. John 16:12 (King James Version); Universal House of Justice, Research Department. "The Unity of Religions in This Century, Jews and the Crucifixion, and the Sacrifice of Ishmael." [n.p.]
5. Armstrong, *A History of God: The 4000-year Quest of Judaism, Christianity, and Islam*, p. 18.
6. The Báb, quoted in Bahá'u'lláh, The Kitáb-i-Íqán, ¶259; Bahá'u'lláh, The Kitáb-i-Íqán, ¶278.
7. 'Abdu'l-Bahá, *Selections from the Writings of 'Abdu'l-Bahá*, no. 31.8.
8. 'Abdu'l-Bahá, *Paris Talks*, no. 29.30–35.
9. Lewis, *The Lion, the Witch and the Wardrobe*, pp. 155, 163.
10. Qur'án 37:102 (Rodwell translation).

11. Bahá'u'lláh, *Gleanings from the Writings of Bahá'u'lláh*, no. 32.1.

12. Genesis 22:11 (New American Standard Bible).

13. Genesis 22:11 (New International Version); Genesis 22:11–12 (King James Version).

14. John 1:29 and Peter 1:19 (King James Version).

15. Shoghi Effendi, *God Passes By*, p. 188; Momen, *An Introduction to Shi'i Islam*, pp. 28–33.

16. Cameron and Momen, *A Basic Bahá'í Chronology*, p. 53.

17. Bowers, *God Speaks Again*, p. 78.

18. Shoghi Effendi, *God Passes By*, p. 298.

16 / A FINAL RESTING PLACE

1. Burns, *Vision of Prophecy*, p. 19.

2. 'Abdu'l-Bahá, *The Promulgation of Universal Peace: Talks Delivered by 'Abdu'l-Bahá during His Visit to the United States and Canada in 1912*, p. 243.

3. Genesis 23:4 (Alter) and Genesis 23:6 (New American Standard Bible).

4. King and Stager, *Life in Biblical Israel*, p. 364.

5. Genesis 23:8–9 (New International Version).

6. Ibid.

7. Genesis 23:11 (New International Version).

8. Genesis 23:13 (New American Standard Bible).

9. Genesis 23:14–15 (New Living Translation).

10. Genesis 23:17 (New American Standard Bible).

11. Ibid.

17 / THREE WEDDINGS AND A FUNERAL

1. Bahá'u'lláh, in *Bahá'í Prayers*, p. 118.

2. Genesis 24:4 (New Living Translation).

3. Genesis 24:10 (New Revised Standard Version).

4. Genesis 24:14 (New Revised Standard Version).

5. Lloyd and Brice, "Harran," p. 83.

6. Genesis 24:17 (New International Version).

7. Genesis 24:18–20 (New International Version).

8. Aruz et al., *Beyond Babylon: Art, Trade, and Diplomacy in the Second Millennium B.C.*, p. 38.

9. Genesis 24:25 (New American Standard Bible).

10. Rappoport, *Myth and Legend of Ancient Israel*, pp. 283–85.

11. Genesis 24:1 (King James Version); Charles, *The Book of Jubilees*, p. 113.

12. Charles, *The Book of Jubilees*, p. 113.

13. Genesis 25:2–4 (King James Version).

14. Genesis 25:6 (King James Version).

15. Hastings, *A Dictionary of the Bible*, p. 509; Eph'al, *The ancient Arabs; Nomads on the Border of the Fertile Crescent 9ᵗʰ–5ᵗʰ Centuries B.C.*, p. 232.

16. Eph'al, *The ancient Arabs; Nomads on the Border of the Fertile Crescent 9ᵗʰ–5ᵗʰ Centuries B.C.*, p. 232; Walton and Matthews, *The IVP Bible Background Commentary*, p. 54.

17. Genesis 13:16 (King James Version).

18. Pringle, *The Churches of the Crusader Kingdom of Jerusalem*, p. 227.

19. Roller, *The Building Program of Herod the Great*, p. 163.

18 / HINTING AT THE FUTURE

1. Winston Churchill, cited in Partington, *Oxford Book of Quotations*, p. 215.

2. Genesis 26:18 (King James Version).

3. Numbers 20:11 (King James Version); John 4:11 (King James Version); the Báb, *Selections from the Writings of the Báb*, 2:14:13; Bahá'u'lláh, *Tablets of Bahá'u'lláh revealed after the Kitáb-i-Aqdas*, p. 212.

4. Deuteronomy 4:24–25 (King James Version).

5. I John 1:5 (King James Version) and John 4:16 (King James Version).

6. Balyuzi, *Muḥammad and the Course of Islam*, pp. 14–15; Qur'án 2:92 (Rodwell translation).

7. Bahá'u'lláh, Epistle to the Son of the Wolf, p. 122; Bahá'u'lláh, The Kitáb-i-Íqán, ¶104.

8. Qur'án 3:90–91 and Qur'án 2:119 (Rodwell translation).

9. Brier and Hobbs, *Daily Life of the Ancient Egyptians*, p. 36.

10. Dietz and McHone, "Kaaba Stone: Not a Meteorite, Probably an Agate," pp. 173–75.

11. Qur'án, page 52, note 125 (Yusuf Ali translation).
12. Lings, *Muḥammad: His Life Based on the Earliest Sources*, p. 4; Siculus, cited in Spicer, *The Ka'bah: Rhythms of Culture, Faith and Physiology*, p. 37.

19 / MOSES

1. 'Abdu'l-Bahá, *Some Answered Questions*, p. 76.
2. Alter, *The Five Books of Moses: A Translations with Commentary*, p. 311.
3. Exodus 2:3–4, in Alter, *The Five Books of Moses: A Translations with Commentary*, p. 312.
4. Exodus 2:7, in Alter, *The Five Books of Moses: A Translation with Commentary*, p. 312.
5. Alter, *The Five Books of Moses: A Translation with Commentary*, p. 312.
6. Exodus 2:11–14 (New International Version).
7. Exodus 2:15 (King James Version).
8. Bahá'u'lláh, The Epistle to the Son of the Wolf, p. 67.
9. Exodus 3:15 (King James Version).
10. Qur'án 6:154 (Rodwell translation); Bahá'u'lláh, The Kitáb-i-Íqán, ¶12.

20 / JESUS THE CHRIST

1. 'Abdu'l-Bahá, *The Promulgation of Universal Peace: Talks Delivered by 'Abdu'l-Bahá during His Visit to the United States and Canada in 1912*, p. 310.
2. Mark 12:26 (King James Version) and Luke 1:54 (New American Standard Bible).
3. John 13:34; Matthew 5:31 (New International Version).
4. 'Abdu'l-Bahá, *Paris Talks*, no. 16.6.
5. Luke 3:38 (King James Version).
6. Micah 5:1–6, Isaiah 11:1, Ezekiel 37:22–26, and 2 Samuel 7:16 (New American Standard Bible).
7. McDonald, *New Catholic Encyclopedia*, p. 319. Two versions of the Catholic Encyclopedia—1913 (Hebermann) and 1967

(McDonald)—agree that there is no valid reason to conclude
that either of the genealogies for Jesus refers to the line of Mary.
An excellent discussion of the difficulties of reconciling the two
genealogies is contained in the 1967 edition, vol. 6, p. 319.

8. A concise explanation of the Islamic point of view is contained
   in the Qur'án 3:33–36, plus the footnote of the Yusuf Ali
   translation. The New Testament mentions the cousinship of Mary
   and Elizabeth in Luke 1:5 and 1:36. The Bahá'í understanding of
   Jesus' descent is found in 'Abdu'l-Bahá, *Some Answered Questions*,
   pp. 63–64.

9. John 18:36 (King James Version); 'Abdu'l-Bahá, *Foundations of World
   Unity*, p. 74.

21 / MUḤAMMAD

1. Qur'án 2:130 (Palmer translation).
2. Psalms 84:6 (King James Version).
3. Deuteronomy 18:18 and Isaiah 42:1–17.
4. John 14:16 (New International Version).
5. John 15:26 (Bible in Basic English).
6. John 16:7 (King James Version).
7. John 14:26 (Douay-Rheims Bible).
8. All of the dialogue and many of the details about Bahira in this
   chapter are taken from Lings, *Muḥammad: His Life Based on the
   Earliest Sources*, pp. 29–30.
9. 'Abdu'l-Bahá, *Some Answered Questions*, p. 13.
10. Qur'án 3:89 (Rodwell translation).
11. Qur'án 2:87 and 3:57 (Palmer translation).
12. Qur'án 5:48, cited in Brown, *A New Introduction to Islam*,
    pp. 231–32.
13. Qur'án 2:256 and 3:19 (Rodwell translation).
14. Extracted on August 26, 2009 from
    http://www.pbs.org/muhammad/m_otherrel.shtml.
15. Genesis 17:20 (King James Version).
16. Qur'án 2:85 (Yusuf Ali translation).
17. Momen, *An Introduction to Shi'i Islam*, pp. 166–70.

22 / THE BÁB

1. Bahá'u'lláh, *Gleanings from the Writings of Bahá'u'lláh*, no. 30.
2. Woodward and Howe, *What hath God wrought: the transformation of America, 1815–1848*, p. 7
3. For a discussion of the sacred writings of the Báb and the laws He promulgated, see Smith, *The Bábí and Bahá'í Religions: From messianic Shi'ism to a world religion*, pp. 31–35.
4. "Mahometan Schism." *London Times*, November 19, 1845. Reproduced on http://the-mission-of-the-bab.blogspot. com/2007_01_01_archive.html.
5. Winter, http://bahai-library.com/winters_chronology_babi_ persecutions.
6. The Báb, *Selections from the Writings of the Báb*, 4:10:6.
7. Ibid., 2:4:3.
8. Nabíl-i-A'zam, *The Dawn-Breakers: Nabil's Narrative of the Early Days of the Bahá'í Revelation*, pp. 76–77.
9. Qur'án 39:68 in Palmer, Rodwell, Yusuf Ali, and others. There is a second verse (79:6–7, Rodwell) that mentions two trumpet blasts, but some translators use the word "trump" or "shock wave" or "commotion" instead of "trumpet."

23 / BAHÁ'U'LLÁH

1. Bahá'u'lláh, *Prayers and Meditations*, p. 20.
2. Ibid., p. 21.
3. Shoghi Effendi, *God Passes By*, pp. 144–50.
4. Ibid., p. 94.
5. The historian who traced the Sasanian Dynasty was Muḥammad Ibn Jarir At-Tabari, who died in AD 922. Also pertinent to the subject of the Sasanian kings is Bailey and Yarshater, *The Cambridge History of Iran*, pp. 697–98. The link between the Nuri family (from which Bahá'u'lláh's father came) and the Sasanian kings is outlined in Balyuzi, *Bahá'u'lláh: The King of Glory*, p. 1.
6. 2 Chronicles 36:22–23 (King James Version).
7. 1 Chronicles 3:19, Matthew 1:12, and Luke 3:27 (New Living

Translation). Jesse is established as King David's father in 'Abdu'l-Bahá, *Some Answered Questions*, pp. 62–63.

8. Boyce, *Zoroastrians: Their Religious Beliefs and Practices*, p. 101.

9. Bahá'u'lláh, The Kitáb-i-Íqán, ¶68, ¶159, ¶12; Bahá'u'lláh, *The Summons of the Lord of Hosts*, "The Súriy-i-Mulúk," no. 15; Bahá'u'lláh, The Kitáb-i-Íqán, ¶159; Bahá'u'lláh, *The Summons of the Lord of Hosts*, "The Súriy-i-Haykal," no. 108.

10. Bahá'u'lláh, The Kitáb-i-Íqán, ¶118, ¶123; Bahá'u'lláh, *Tablets of Bahá'u'lláh revealed after the Kitáb-i-Aqdas*, p. 124; Bahá'u'lláh, Epistle to the Son of the Wolf, p. 166; Bahá'u'lláh, *Gleanings from the Writings of Bahá'u'lláh*, no. 135.2.

11. Bahá'u'lláh, *Gleanings from the Writings of Bahá'u'lláh*, no. 22.1, 34.5.

12. Ibid., no. 54.1, no. 131.2.

13. Micah 7:12 (King James Version).

24 / IDENTIFYING ABRAHAM'S DESCENDANTS

1. Bahá'u'lláh, The Hidden Words, Arabic no. 68.

2. Shreeve, "The Greatest Journey Ever Told: The Trail of Our DNA," p. 62.

3. Olson, "The Royal We," pp. 62–64.

4. Ibid., p. 63.

5. Ibid., p. 64.

6. Genesis 13:16 (King James Version).

25 / PROPHECY FULFILLED

1. Kung, in a speech given at Santa Clara University on March 31, 2005, http://www.scu.edu/ethics/practicing/focusareas/global_ethics/laughlin-lectures/kung-world-religions.html.

2. 'Abdu'l-Bahá, *The Promulgation of Universal Peace: Talks Delivered by 'Abdu'l-Bahá During His Visit to the United States and Canada in 1912*, p. 513.

3. Dosick, *Living Judaism: the complete guide to Jewish belief, tradition and practice*, p. 67.

4. Mark 3:34–35 (New Revised Standard Version).

5. Qur'án 2:112 (Yusuf Ali translation).
6. Wikipedia article: http://en.wikipedia.org/wiki/Parliament_of_the_ World's_Religions.
7. Hanson, *The world's congress of religions,* pp. 950–51.

Appendix A: But What about Other Religions?

1. 'Abdu'l-Bahá, *The Promulgation of Universal Peace: Talks Delivered by 'Abdu'l-Bahá during His Visit to the United States and Canada in 1912,* pp. 209–10.
2. John 10:16 (King James Version).
3. Holder, *The Blackwell Companion to Christian Spirituality,* p. 163.
4. Contributed by Prithvi Vinod. Further information can be found in his book *19,000 Years of World History,* written under the pen name Prithviraj R.
5. Vinod, http://prithvithoughts.blogspot.com/.
6. Neusner, "Note on Barukh ben Neriah and Zoroaster," p. 359; 'Abdu'l-Bahá, *Some Answered Questions,* p. 213. Some of these alleged connections are more fully described in "Biblical Memoranda," an article (no author listed) in *The Quarterly Theological Review and Ecclesiastical Record,* v.2, 1825, pp. 193–94.
7. Nelson, *Buddha: His Life and His Teaching,* pp. 16–17.

Appendix B: The Ancient Sabean Faith and Sabeanism Today

1. Mandaean Root.com, http://www.mandaeanroot.com/.
2. Land-Poole, Stanley, *Studies in a Mosque,* http//books.google.com.
3. Hornby, *Lights of Guidance,* no. 1694.
4. *Science,* 3/8/2007, vol. 317, pp. 588, 589.

BIBLIOGRAPHY

WORKS OF BAHÁ'U'LLÁH

Epistle to the Son of the Wolf. Wilmette, IL: Bahá'í Publishing Trust, 1988.

Gleanings from the Writings of Bahá'u'lláh. Wilmette, IL: Bahá'í Publishing, 2005.

The Hidden Words. Translated by Shoghi Effendi. Wilmette, IL: Bahá'í Publishing, 2002.

The Kitáb-i-Íqán: The Book of Certitude. Translated by Shoghi Effendi. Wilmette, IL: Bahá'í Publishing, 2003.

Prayers and Meditations by Bahá'u'lláh. Translated by Shoghi Effendi. 1st ps ed. Wilmette, IL: Bahá'í Publishing Trust, 1987.

The Summons of the Lord of Hosts: Tablets of Bahá'u'lláh. Wilmette, IL: Bahá'í Publishing, 2006.

Tablets of Bahá'u'lláh revealed after the Kitáb-i-Aqdas. Compiled by the Research Department of the Universal House of Justice. Translated by Habib Taherzadeh et al. Wilmette, IL: Bahá'í Publishing Trust, 1988.

WORKS OF THE BÁB

Selections from the Writings of the Báb. Compiled by the Research Department of the Universal House of Justice. Translated by Habib Taherzadeh et al. Wilmette, IL: Bahá'í Publishing Trust, 2006.

WORKS OF 'ABDU'L-BAHÁ

Foundations of World Unity. Wilmette, IL: Bahá'í Publishing Trust, 1972.

Paris Talks. Wilmette, IL: Bahá'í Publishing, 2006.

The Promulgation of Universal Peace: Talks Delivered by 'Abdu'l-Bahá during His Visit to the United States and Canada in 1912. Wilmette, IL: Bahá'í Publishing Trust, 2007.

Selections from the Writings of 'Abdu'l-Bahá. Wilmette, IL: Bahá'í Publishing, 2010.

Some Answered Questions. Compiled and translated by Laura Clifford
Barney. 1ˢᵗ pocket-size ed. Wilmette, IL: Bahá'í Publishing Trust,
1984.

WORKS OF SHOGHI EFFENDI

Arohanui: Letters from Shoghi Effendi to New Zealand. Suva, Fiji: Bahá'í
Publishing Trust, 1982.

Bahá'í Administration: Selected Letters 1922–1932. 5ᵗʰ ed. Wilmette, IL:
Bahá'í Publishing Trust, 1968.

Dawn of a New Day. New Delhi: Bahá'í Publishing Trust, [n.d.].

God Passes By. Revised ed. Seventh printing. Wilmette, IL: Bahá'í
Publishing Trust, 1994.

Letters from the Guardian to Australia and New Zealand. Paddington
[N.S.W.]: National Spiritual Assembly of the Bahá'ís of Australia.
Electronic version downloaded from http://www.bahai-education.
org/ocean.

The Promised Day is Come. 1ˢᵗ pocket-size ed. Wilmette, IL: Bahá'í
Publishing Trust, 1996.

COMPILATIONS

Bahá'u'lláh, the Báb, and 'Abdu'l-Bahá. *Bahá'í Prayers: A Selection of
Prayers Revealed by Bahá'u'lláh, the Báb, and 'Abdu'l-Bahá.* New ed.
Wilmette, IL: Bahá'í Publishing Trust, 2002.

Helen Hornby, comp. *Lights of Guidance.* New ed. New Delhi: Bahá'í
Publishing Trust, 1999.

TRANSLATIONS OF THE BIBLE AND TORAH

Alter, Robert. *The Five Books of Moses: A Translation with Commentary.*
New York: W. W. Norton & Co., 2004.

Bible in Basic English. http://basicenglishbible.com/.

Cook, Frederic Charles. *The Holy Bible, According to the Authorized
Version (A.D. 1611).* Volume 1, Part 1. New York: Charles Scribners,
1896. http://books.google.com.

Douay-Rheims Bible. http://drb.scripturetext.com/isiah/60.htm.

King James Version. http://kingjbible.com/genesis/1.htm.

New American Standard Bible. http://nasb.scripturetext.com/.

New International Version. http://niv.scripturetext.com/.

New Living Translation. http://www.biblegateway.com/.

New Revised Standard Version. http://www.devotions.net/home.htm.

Scharfstein, Sol. *Torah and Commentary.* Jersey City: KTAV Publishing House, 2008.

Smith, Julia E., trans. *The Holy Bible: Containing the Old and New Testaments.* Hartford: American Publishing Company, 1876. http://books.google.com.

World English Bible. http://worldebible.com.

Young, Robert, trans. *Young's Literal Translation of the Bible.* 1898. http://yltbible.com.

TRANSLATIONS OF THE QUR'ÁN

Palmer, E. H., trans. *The Qur'án.* Oxford: Clarendon Press, 1849. Electronic version downloaded from http://www.bahai-education.org/ocean.

Pickthall, Mohammad Marmaduke. *The Meaning of the Glorious Qur'án: An explanatory translation.* New York and Toronto: The New American Library (A Mentor Religious Classic), 11th printing [n.d.].

Rodwell, J. M., trans. *The Qur'án.* Electronic version downloaded from http://www.bahai-education.org/ocean.

Turner, Colin, trans. *The Qur'án, a New Interpretation.* Richmond, England: Curzon Press, 1997.

Yusuf Ali, A., trans. *The Qur'án.* Electronic version downloaded from http://www.bahai-education.org/ocean.

OTHER SOURCES

American Urological Association, http://urologyhealth.org/pediatric/index.cfm?cat=10&topic=350.

Armstrong, Karen. *A History of God: The 4000-year Quest of Judaism, Christianity, and Islam.* New York: Ballantine, 1994.

Aruz, Joan et al., eds. *Beyond Babylon: Art, Trade, and Diplomacy in the Second Millennium B.C.* New Haven: Yale University Press, 2008.

At-Tabari, Muhammad Ibn-Garir. *The History of Al-Tabari.* Vol. 4, *The Ancient Kingdoms.* Translated and annotated by Moshe Perlmann. Albany: State University of New York Press, 1987.

Bailey, Harold, and Ehsan Yarshater. *The Cambridge History of Iran.* Vol. 3. Cambridge: Cambridge University Press, 1983.

Balyuzi, H. M. *Bahá'u'lláh: The King of Glory*. Oxford: George Ronald, 1991.

———. *Muḥammad and the Course of Islam*. Oxford: George Ronald, 1976.

Baring-Gould, Sabine. *Legends of the Patriarchs and Prophets and Other Old Testament Characters from Various Sources*. New York: W. L. Allison, 1882. http://books.google.com.

Becking, Bob, Meindert Dijkstra, and Karel J. H. Vriezen. *Only One God? Monotheism in Ancient Israel and the Veneration of the Goddess Asherah*. London: Sheffield Academic Press, 2001. http://books.google.com.

"The Beehive Enigma," http://www.saudiaramcoworld.com/issue/196706/the.beehive.enigma.htm.

Bialik, Hayyim Nahman, andYehoshua Hana Rawnitzki. *Sefer Ha-Aggadah: The Book of Jewish Folklore and Legend*. Selected, translated, and annotated by Chaim Pear. Tel Aviv: Dvir, 1988.

Bliss, Carmen, ed. *The World's Best Poetry*. Vol. 1. Great Neck, NY: Granger Book Co., Inc., 1981.

Bowers, Kenneth. *God Speaks Again*. Wilmette, IL: Bahá'í Publishing, 2004.

Boyce, Mary. *Zoroastrians: Their Religious Beliefs and Practices*. New York: Routledge, 2001.

Bremmer, Jan N. *The Strange World of Human Sacrifice*. Dudley, MA: Peeters, 2007.

Brier, Bob, and A. Hoyt Hobbs. *Daily Life of the Ancient Egyptians*. Westport, CT: Greenwood Press, 1999.

Brown, Daniel W. *A New Introduction to Islam*. Malden, MA: Blackwell Pub., 2003.

Bukhari, Muhammad ibn Ismail, comp. *The Hadith of Bukhari*. 8 vols. http://www.bahai-education.org/ocean.

Bulliet, Richard W. *The Camel and the Wheel*. New York: Columbia University Press, 1990.

Burns, James D. *Vision of Prophecy*. 2nd edition. London: James Nisbet and Co., 1865. http://books.google.com.

Cameron, Glenn, with Wendi Momen. *A Basic Bahá'í Chronology*. Oxford: George Ronald, 1996.

Charles, R. H., trans. *The Book of Jubilees*. New York: Cosimo, 2003. http://books.google.com.

Collinson, Diane, Kathryn Plant, and Robert Wilkinson. *Fifty Eastern Thinkers.* London: Routledge, 2000. http://books.google.com.

Conacher, A. J., and Maria Sala. *Land Degradation in Mediterranean Environments of the World.* Chichester, New York: Wiley, 1998. http://books.google.com.

Curatola, Giovanni, ed. *The Art and Architecture of Mesopotamia.* New York: Abbeville Press, 2006.

Darr, Shaheen. "The miracle of Zam Zam water." http://www.helium.com/items/1052721-the-miracle-of-zam-zam-water.

Deiss, Lucien, and Madeleine Beaumont. *Joseph, Mary, Jesus.* Collegeville, MN: Liturgical Press, 1996.

Dietz, Robert S., and John McHone. "Kaaba Stone: Not a Meteorite, Probably an Agate." *Meteoritics* 9, no. 2 (June, 1974): 173–75. http://adsabs.harvard.edu/abs/1974Metic...9..173D.

Denniston, George C., Frederick Mansfield Hodges, and Marilyn Fayre Milos, eds. *Male and Female Circumcision: Medical, Legal, and Ethical Considerations in Pediatric Practice.* New York: Kluwer Academic / Plenum Publishers, 1999.

Dosick, Wayne D. *Living Judaism: The Complete Guide to Jewish Belief, Tradition, and Practice.* New York: Harper, 1995. http://books.google.com.

Dumper, Michael, and Bruce Stanley, eds. *Cities of the Middle East and North Africa: A Historical Encyclopedia.* Santa Barbara, CA: ABC-CLIO, 2007. http://books.google.com.

Elwell, Walter A., and Philip W. Comfort. *Tyndale Bible Dictionary.* Wheaton, IL: Tyndale House Publishers, 2001.

Enzel, Yehouda, Amotz Agnon, and Mordechai Stein. *New Frontiers in Dead Sea Paleoenvironmental Research.* Boulder, CO: Geological Society of America, 2006. http://books.google.com.

Eph'al, Israel. *The Ancient Arabs: Nomads on the Border of the Fertile Crescent 9th–5th Centuries B.C.* Jerusalem: Magnes Press, The Hebrew University, 1984. http://books.google.com.

Evans, Bergen, ed. *Dictionary of Quotations.* New York: Delacorte Press, 1968.

Falk, Avner. *A Psychoanalytic History of the Jews.* Cranbury, NJ: Associated University Presses, 1996.

Finkelstein, Israel, and Neil Asher Silberman. *The Bible Unearthed.* New York: The Free Press, 2001.

Forbes, R. J. *Studies in Ancient Technology.* Vol. 1. Leiden: E. J. Brill, 1993.

Freedman, David Noel, Allen C. Myers, and Astrid B. Beck. *Eerdmans Dictionary of the Bible.* Grand Rapids, MI: Wm. B. Eerdmans Publishing, 2000.

Ginzburg, Louis. *The Legends of the Jews.* Vol. I. Translated by Henrietta Szold. Baltimore, MD: Johns Hopkins University Press, 1998.

Gollaher, David. *Circumcision: A History of the World's Most Controversial Surgery.* New York: Basic Books, 2001.

Gonen, Rivka. *Contested Holiness: Jewish, Muslim, and Christian Perspectives on the Temple Mount in Jerusalem.* Jersey City, NJ: KTAV Publishing House, 2003. http://books.google.com.

——. *Burial Patterns and Cultural Diversity in Bronze-Age Canaan.* Winona Lake, IN: Eisenbrauns, 1992. http://books.google.com.

Green, Tamara M. *The City of the Moon God: Religious Traditions of Harran.* Leiden: E. J. Brill, 1992.

Hanson, J. W. *The world's congress of religions.* Chicago: International Publishing Co., 1894. http://books.google.com.

Harris, Rivkah. *Gender and Aging in Mesopotamia: The Gilgamesh Epic and Other Ancient Literature.* Norman: University of Oklahoma Press, 2000. http://books.google.com.

Hastings, James, ed. *A Dictionary of the Bible.* Vol. 4. Honolulu: University Press of the Pacific, 2004. http://books.google.com.

Henry, Carl Ferdinand Howard. *God, Revelation, and Authority.* Vol. 1. Wheaton, IL: Crossway, 1999. http://books.google.com.

Herbermann, Charles G., Condé Pallen, and Thomas Shahan, eds. *The Catholic Eycyclopedia.* Vol. 6. New York: Gilmary Society, 1913.

Hillel, Daniel. *The Natural History of the Bible.* New York: Columbia University Press, 2006.

Holley, Horace. *Bahai: The Spirit of the Age.* New York: Brentano's Publishers, 1921.

Horowitz, Wayne. *Mesopotamian Cosmic Geography.* Winona Lake, IN: Eisenbrauns, 1998.

"In the Marshes of Iraq." Saudi Aramco World, Nov / Dec 1966. [n.p.] http://www.saudiaramcoworld.com/issue/196606/in.the.marshes.of.iraq.htm.

Jenkins, D. T. *The Cambridge History of Western Textiles.* Cambridge: Cambridge University Press, 2003. http://books.google.com.

King, Philip J., and Lawrence E. Stager. *Life in Biblical Israel.*
Louisville: Westminster John Knox Press, 2001.

Klinghoffer, David. *The Discovery of God.* New York: Doubleday, 2003.

Kung, Hans. Speech given at Santa Clara University on March 31,
2005. http://www.scu.edu/ethics/practicing/focusareas/global_
ethics/laughlin-lectures/kung-world-religions.html.

LaFraniere, Sharon. "Circumcision Studied in Africa as Aids
Preventative." *New York Times.* Page A1, col. 3, April 28, 2006.

Land-Poole, Stanley. *Studies in a Mosque.* London: Eden, Remington
& Co, 1893. http//books.google.com.

Langenheim, Jean H. *Plant Resins: Chemistry, Evolution, Ecology,
Ethnobotany.* Portland, OR: Timber Press, 2003. http://books.
google.com.

Lawler, Andrew. "Middle Asia Takes Center Stage." *Science* 317 (August
3, 2007): 586–90.

Lawrence, Thomas Edward. *The Diary Kept by T. E. Lawrence While
Travelling in Arabia During 1911.* Reading, England: Garnet / Ithaca
Press, 1993.

Leeming, David A. *Jealous Gods and Chosen People.* Oxford: Oxford
University Press, 2004.

Lewis, Clive Staples. *The Lion, the Witch and the Wardrobe.* New York:
HarperCollins, 1978.

Lings, Martin. *Muḥammad: His Life Based on the Earliest Sources.*
Rochester, VT: Inner Traditions International, 1983.

Lloyd, Seton, and William Brice. "Harran." *Anatolian Studies* 1 (1951):
77–111.

Maalouf, Tony. *Arabs in the Shadow of Israel.* Grand Rapids, MI:
Kregel Publications, 2003. http://books.google.com.

"Mahometan Schism." *London Times.* November 19, 1845. Reproduced
on http://the-mission-of-the-bab.blogspot.com/2007_01_01_
archive.html.

Matthews, Gary. *Every Eye Shall See: Bible Evidence for the Return of
Christ.* Knoxville, TN: Stonehaven Press, 1999.

McDonald, William J., editor-in-chief. *New Catholic Encyclopedia.* Vol.
6, *Fra-Hir.* New York: McGraw Hill, 1967.

Miller, James Maxwell, and John Haralson Hayes. *A History of Ancient
Israel and Judah.* Louisville, KY: Westminster John Knox Press, 1986.

Mir, Muhammad. *Understanding the Islamic Scripture: A Study of Selected Passages from the Qur'án.* New York: Pearson Longman, 2008.

Momen, Moojan. *An Introduction to Shi'i Islam.* Oxford: George Ronald Press, 1985.

Momen, Wendi. *A Basic Bahá'í Dictionary.* Oxford: George Ronald Press, 1989.

Monger, George P. *Marriage Customs of the World: From Henna to Honeymoons.* Santa Barbara, CA: ABC-CLIO, 2004. http://books.google.com.

Nabíl-i-A'zam. [Muhammad-i-Zarandí]. *The Dawn-Breakers: Nabíl's Narrative of the Early Days of the Bahá'í Revelation.* Translated and edited by Shoghi Effendi. Wilmette, IL: Bahá'í Publishing Trust, 1932.

Nelson, Walter Henry. *Buddha: His Life and His Teaching.* New York: Jeremy P. Tarcher / Penguin, 2008.

Nemet-Najat, Karen Rhea. *Daily Life in Ancient Mesopotamia.* Peabody, MA: Hendrickson Publishers, 1998.

Neusner, Jacob. "Note on Barukh ben Neriah and Zoroaster." *Journal of the American Academy of Religion* 32:4 (1964): 359–60.

Oden, Robert A., Jr. "The Persistence of Canaanite Religion." *The Biblical Archaeologist* 39:1 (March, 1976): 31–36.

Olson, Steve. "The Royal We." *Atlantic Monthly* 289:5 (May, 2002): 62–64.

Osborne, Grant, and Philip W. Comfort. *Life Application Bible Commentary: Hebrews.* Wheaton, IL: Tyndale, 2000. http://books.google.com.

Partington, Angela, ed. *Oxford Book of Quotations.* Rev. ed. Oxford: Oxford University Press, 1992.

Plaut, Gunther, and David E. Stein. *The Torah: A Modern Commentary.* New York: URJ Press, 2005.

Pringle, Denys. *The Churches of the Crusader Kingdom of Jerusalem.* Vol 1. Cambridge: Cambridge University Press, 1993.

R., Prithviraj. *19,000 Years of World History: The Story of Religion.* Lulu.com, 2008.

Rapp, George Robert. *Archaeomineralogy.* Berlin: Springer, 2002. http://books.google.com.

Rappoport, Angelo S. *Myth and Legend of Ancient Israel.* Vol. 1. Whitefish, MT: Kessinger Publishing, 1928.

Roller, Duane W. *The Building Program of Herod the Great.* Los Angeles: University of California Press, 1998. http://books.google.com.

Rolleston, Frances. *Mazzaroth; or, the Constellations.* London: Rivingtons, 1862. http://books.google.com.

Saxon, Elizabeth. *The Eucharist in Romanesque France: Iconography and Theology.* Woodbridge: Boydell Press, 2006. http://books.google.com.

Scarre, Chris, editor-in-chief. *Smithsonian Timelines of the Ancient World.* Washington, DC: Smithsonian Institution, 1993.

Segal, Alan F. *Life After Death: A History of the Afterlife in the Religions of the West.* New York: Random House, 2004.

Sheridan, Mark, ed. *Genesis 12–50.* Vol. II. Downers Grove, IL: InterVarsity Press, 2002.

Shreeve, James. "The Greatest Journey Ever Told: The Trail of Our DNA." *National Geographic Magazine* 209:3 (March, 2006): 60–69.

Shurcliff, Arthur A. *A Man Walks the Earth: Near and Far in New England.* Boston: The Old Corner Book Store, 1951.

Silver, Abba Hillel. *History of Messianic Speculation in Israel.* Whitefish MT: Kessinger Publishing, 2003.

Smith, Peter. *The Bábí and Bahá'í Religions: From Messianic Shi'ism to a World Religion.* Cambridge: Cambridge University Press, 1987.

Spencer, Michael. "The Marsh Arabs Revisited." *Saudi Aramco World* (March / April 1982). http://www.saudiaramcoworld.com/issue/198202/the.marsh.arabs.revisited.htm.

Spicer, Beverly White. *The Ka'bah: Rhythms of Culture, Faith and Physiology.* Lanham, MD: University Press of America, 2003. http://books.google.com.

Stanton, Elizabeth Cady. *The Woman's Bible.* New York: European Publishing Company, 1895. http://books.google.com.

Strouhal, Evzen, and Werner Forman. *Life of the Ancient Egyptians.* Norman: University of Oklahoma Press, 1992.

Swedenborg, Emmanuel. *The Apocalypse Explained According to the Spiritual Sense.* Vol. II. New York: American Swedenborg Printing and Publishing Society, 1892. http://books.google.com.

Szulc, Tad. Photos by Reza. "Journey of Faith." Pages 1–5 accessed online at http://ngm.nationalgeographic.com/features/world/asia/israel/abraham-text/1.

Taherzadeh, Adib. *The Revelation of Bahá'u'lláh*. 4 vols. Oxford: George Ronald, 1974.

Task Force on Circumcision. "Circumcision Policy Statement." *Pediatrics* 103:3 (March 1999): 686–93. http://pediatrics. aappublications.org/cgi/content/full/103/3/686.

Thoreau, Henry David. *Walden and Other Writings of Henry David Thoreau.* Edited by Brooks Atkinson. New York: Random House, 1965.

Townsend, George. *The Heart of the Gospel.* London: George Ronald, 1960.

Turner, Harold W. *From Temple to Meeting House.* The Hague: Mouton, 1979.

Universal House of Justice, Research Department. "The Unity of Religions in This Century, Jews and the Crucifixion, and the Sacrifice of Ishmael." Memorandum dated 24 October, 1990. http://bahai-library.com/file.php?file=uhj_unity_religions_jews_ishmael.

Vermes, Geza. *Post-biblical Jewish Studies.* Leiden: E. J. Brill, 1975. http://books.google.com.

Walters, T. F. "The Beehive Enigma." *Saudi Aramco World.* Nov / Dec 1967. http://www.saudiaramcoworld.com/issue/196706/the.beehive. enigma.htm.

Walton, John H., and Victor Harold Matthews. *The IVP Bible Background Commentary.* Downer's Grove, IL: Intervarsity Press, 1997. http://books.google.com.

Watson, Noelle, Trudy Ring, and Paul Schellinger. *International Dictionary of Historical Places: Middle East and Africa.* Chicago: Fitzroy Dearborn, 1996.

Wiesel Elie. *Wise Men and Their Tales: Portraits of Biblical, Talmudic, and Hasidic Masters.* New York: Schocken, 2003.

Wikipedia. "Parliament of the World's Religions." http://en.wikipedia. org/wiki/Parliament_of_the_World's_Religions.

Winters, Jonah. "Chronology of persecutions of Bábis and Bahá'ís." http://bahai-library.com/resources/chronology.bahai.html.

Woodward, Comer Vann, and Daniel Walker Howe. *What hath God wrought: the transformation of America, 1815–1848.* New York: Oxford University Press, 2007.

Young, Dwight W. "A Mathematical Approach to Certain Dynastic Spans in the Sumerian King List." *Journal of Near Eastern Studies* 47:2 (April, 1998): 123–29.

INDEX

Bahá'í
PUBLISHING
AND THE BAHÁ'Í FAITH

Bahá'í Publishing produces books based on the teachings of the Bahá'í Faith. Founded over 160 years ago, the Bahá'í Faith has spread to some 235 nations and territories and is now accepted by more than five million people. The word "Bahá'í" means "follower of Bahá'u'lláh." Bahá'u'lláh, the founder of the Bahá'í Faith, asserted that He is the Messenger of God for all of humanity in this day. The cornerstone of His teachings is the establishment of the spiritual unity of humankind, which will be achieved by personal transformation and the application of clearly identified spiritual principles. Bahá'ís also believe that there is but one religion and that all the Messengers of God—among them Abraham, Zoroaster, Moses, Krishna, Buddha, Jesus, and Muḥammad—have progressively revealed its nature. Together, the world's great religions are expressions of a single, unfolding divine plan. Human beings, not God's Messengers, are the source of religious divisions, prejudices, and hatreds.

The Bahá'í Faith is not a sect or denomination of another religion, nor is it a cult or a social movement. Rather, it is a globally recognized independent world religion founded on new books of scripture revealed by Bahá'u'lláh.

Bahá'í Publishing is an imprint of the National Spiritual Assembly of the Bahá'ís of the United States.

For more information about the Bahá'í Faith,
or to contact Bahá'ís near you,
visit http://www.bahai.us/
or call
1-800-22-UNITE

OTHER BOOKS AVAILABLE FROM
BAHÁ'Í PUBLISHING

Zanján
Aaron Emmel with illustrations by C. Aaron Kreader
$12.00 U.S. / $14.00 CAN
Trade Paper
ISBN 978-1-931847-88-9

Zanján is a rich fictional work that is based on actual events from one of the many dramatic episodes surrounding the emergence of the Bahá'í Faith in mid-nineteenth century Persia. In this story, Navid has been trained from an early age to join the elite, but everything he learns only leads him to more questions. His search for answers will take him from the quiet village where he grew up to the greatest cities of nineteenth-century Persia, and ultimately into the middle of a war that will tear apart families, challenge the country's most powerful leaders, and force Navid to question everything that he thought he knew. As the imperial army clashes with scholars and peasants in the ancient streets of Zanján, Navid will participate in the birth of a new spiritual movement that has the power to transform the world.

Spirit of Faith
THE ONENESS OF HUMANITY
Bahá'í Publishing
$12.00 U.S. / $14.00 CAN
Hardcover
ISBN 978-1-931847-86-5

Spirit of Faith: The Oneness of Humanity is a compilation of writings and prayers that offer a glimpse of the extensive Bahá'í writings concerning the oneness of humanity. Like the titles that have come before it, this collection of sacred scripture underscores the unity of thought that helps us define our place within a single, unfolding, divine creation. The Spirit of Faith series continues to explore spiritual topics—such as the oneness of religion, the eternal covenant of God, the promise of world peace, and more—by presenting what the central figures of the Bahá'í Faith have written regarding these important topics. It is hoped that readers of all faiths will find passages here that help them meditate and reflect on how we can all take steps to improve the world through love, unity, and collaboration.

Talks by 'Abdu'l-Bahá
UNIVERSAL EDUCATION
'Abdu'l-Bahá
$14.00 U.S. / $16.00 CAN
Hardcover
ISBN 978-1-931847-87-2

Talks by 'Abdu'l-Bahá: Universal Education continues the series of talks given by 'Abdu'l-Bahá—the son and appointed successor of Bahá'u'lláh, the Prophet and Founder of the Bahá'í Faith—during his historic journey through Europe and North America in 1911 and 1912. 'Abdu'l-Bahá's talks continue to offer profound direction and insight into many of the world's most challenging issues. This volume considers the vital topic of education and its importance in this era. Central to the principles of the Bahá'í Faith is the pronouncement that all mankind should be afforded access to an education—this includes both a material education for the furthering of sciences and trades, as well as mankind's spiritual education, which is being advanced to a level of maturity unseen in previous ages.

Paris Talks
ADDRESSES GIVEN BY 'ABDU'L-BAHÁ IN 1911
'Abdu'l-Bahá
$21.00 U.S. / $23.00 CAN
Hardcover
ISBN 978-1-931847-90-2

Paris Talks documents the extraordinary series of inspiring and up-lifting public addresses 'Abdu'l-Bahá gave on his historic visit to Paris in the early twentieth century. Despite advanced age and poor health, he set out from Palestine in 1911 on a momentous journey to Europe and North America to share the teachings and vision of the Bahá'í Faith with the people of the West.

Addressing such subjects as the nature of humankind, the soul, the Prophets of God, the establishment of world peace, the abolition of all forms of prejudice, the equality of women and men, the harmony of science and religion, the causes of war, and many other subjects, 'Abdu'l-Bahá spoke in a profound yet simple manner that transcended social and cultural barriers. His deep spiritual wisdom remains as timely and soul-stirring as it was a century ago.